The Conspirator Who Saved the Romanovs

THE
CONSPIRATOR
WHO
SAVED
THE
ROMANOVS

GARY NULL

PRENTICE-HALL, INC.
Englewood Cliffs, New Jersey

ACKNOWLEDGMENTS

Steve Null, who traveled around this country and in Europe collecting information and photographs; Sarah Dona, who helped in the editing of the final draft; Tom Croft, Steve Wieder, Ron McCulty, Stan Slapin, Ron Milkie, John Lee, George Marcus and Nick Carrado, Jr., who all assisted in giving me valuable information without which I would not have completed the book; John Petrigac, James Dawson, and Jerry Krutman, who assisted in the editing, fact collecting and helped me sort through miles of data to come up with the few necessary facts; Rick Shulman, who labored through several drafts of typing; Rick Moody, who translated French, German and Russian; Jim Bove, who was most significant for assisting with some of the stylizing, creative editing and general consultation on the manuscript; and most of all, to Rose Bently, who gave me the original idea and thus made it all possible.

CONTENTS

The Conspirator Who Saved the Romanovs

ONE

PROLOGUE

The incredible story of Aaron Simanovitsch was first brought to my attention by his niece, Rose Bently. My first reaction was one of disbelief. Could a member of the most directly persecuted minority in Tsarist Russia not only achieve the contacts and financial means to become a pivotal figure in the Court of Nicholas II, but actually use his power unselfishly? Could anyone in this period actually have saved thousands of his fellow Russian Jews from the inhuman vagaries of the Tsar's armies and the remorselessness of so-called Russian justice? Could the Imperial Family have accepted him as the unofficial minister for the Jews in a dark moment of their history? Was it possibly true that this man had been a central figure in the escape of the last Romanovs, supposedly executed at Ekaterinburg so long ago? Men such as this were surely creations of historical fiction.

But the more I investigated, the more vividly the story constructed itself for me. Not only were the general outlines verifiable, but manifold details appeared which proved that in a century of untold political wickedness, one Aaron Simanovitsch had indeed managed to construct a machinery of gigantic dimensions and complexity to be used for the good of his people. And, this, with the aid of the most inscrutable, most despised, most scandalized and feared public figure in Russian history: the enigmatic Russian *starets*, Father Grigori—known to the world as Rasputin, "the Defiled One."

In 1919 Aaron Simanovitsch had come to America. When he

1

returned to Europe, he left behind an attaché case containing letters, a journal, and a manuscript describing in detail what it had been like to be a Jew in the Imperial Court. Simanovitsch, who realized that his numerous intrigues on behalf of the Jews, which continued until his death in 1941, might cause him to fall victim to sudden death or disappearance, instructed a friend to reveal the contents of the attaché case if any such thing happened. But Simanovitsch did not meet such a fate. Many of the events related in this book are taken from the manuscripts in the attaché case, which, for various reasons, still remain unseen and unpublished.

The events were corroborated through additional sources, however, and supplemented over a period of two years, during which time I interviewed over two hundred historians, scholars, and investigators, many of whom had access to information never before made public. At last, the full story was uncovered, concealed as it had been by a web of protective intrigue woven for the sake of the many who risked their lives and fortunes to aid Simanovitsch's ventures.

The various leaders of the Jewish community did not idly choose Simanovitsch to act as a liaison between them and the Court. Never before in their history had a Jew risen to such heights: he served as jeweler for the Imperial Court and as the private secretary, tutor, and confidant of Rasputin. Their choice proved a wise one, for in his rise to become the most powerful Jew in Russia, Simanovitsch spared no pains to protect them with the utmost discretion and secrecy.

Among numerous other accomplishments, Simanovitsch brought the Jewish theater out of the ghettoes, developed technical schools for youths arbitrarily deprived of a higher education, and kept no less than five thousand Jews from serving in the Tsar's army during the First World War. Simanovitsch always operated to the extreme limits of his powers and was in constant danger of his life; if he had permitted his methods of operation to be known, he would not have been able to develop the international network that financed and assisted Russian and German Jewish refugees, businessmen, and students. Although he was not personally responsible, it is no exaggeration to say that Simanovitsch certainly played a major role in helping create the climate of opinion which stimulated the

Bolsheviks to make the first article in their new constitution a demand for equality for the Jewish people of Russia.

With the current restimulation of interest in the Imperial Family, it is appropriate that Simanovitsch's story now be told. In all of Russian history, there was possibly never a more intriguing—in both senses of the word—and complex pair than Rasputin and Simanovitsch; their combined weight in the balance of history is incalculable.

These, then, are the facts that I have uncovered, having exhausted all possible information and having reduced the historical descriptions and contradictions to the absolute minimum, given the ambiguity of this era of history. Now and again I have had to disrupt the chronology of the narrative and move backward and forward in time in order to put events into their proper perspective.

Owing to the delicate nature of this material, the names of many persons who have thoughtfully offered their time and energy to bring this book to light have been respectfully withheld, as promised. Certain manuscripts, which I am not at liberty to divulge, have been utilized, and the conditions of discretion under which I have been able to study these manuscripts have also been respected.

Americans who have believed the story of the bloody execution of the Romanov Family should now weigh the evidence presented both in this book and in Guy Richards' *The Hunt for the Czar* (Garden City, N.Y.: Doubleday, 1970). The details of the well-hidden escape are only now coming to light in the American, Canadian, and British press. For the first time, the details of Simanovitsch's vast intelligence network will be generally accessible.

But perhaps more important than Simanovitsch's intrigues of the Russian Court in the last days of the Tsars, or his unbelievable partnership with Rasputin, or the ingenuity and frustrations of the escape from Ekaterinburg, is the evidence that one man, without title or official political position, could shoulder the responsibility for accomplishing untold good and fight a Holy War against the oppression of his people, while empires and nations fell into chaos around him.

Gary Null
New York City

TWO

One October morning, early in this century, as the air sharpened itself under the gray Russian sky, Aaron Simanovitsch waited on the platform for the train that would take him from Kiev to St. Petersburg. The train was late, but he could well afford to endure the delay. He was about to launch himself into that greater world of men, the Imperial capital.

It wasn't that this lesser, provincial world had held nothing for him; his journey was not an escape from failure. On the contrary, he had prospered here in Kiev, had gathered its offerings and opportunities with zest, and had built for himself a solid livelihood in the buying and selling of jewels. He had succeeded domestically too: his wife, the daughter of a prominent contractor, had set up with him a household which he could be proud of. But some men find pride to be a vapid commodity, and Aaron Simanovitsch was just such a man. A germ of restlessness swam in his being and prodded him to the point of decision. He would never be satisfied unless he had tested himself in the great lake of Russian society, St. Petersburg.

But the move meant he had to leave his family, for perhaps as long as three years, and he did not like this separation. He didn't at all like the position of Jews in the Russia of Nicholas II, and he was uncertain about leaving his family unprotected.

When he reached St. Petersburg, Simanovitsch immediately began the arduous task of setting up a business in a new territory. He was not entirely alone, however, for his wife had numerous relatives here. They were solid tradesmen and merchants—modest, hard-working folk whose greatest achievement consisted of a few commissions from the Imperial Court. They were very pleased to hear from Simanovitsch and offered him all sorts of help in settling down. Of course they would put him up until he found a place of his own. And would he like to be introduced to Mr. ———? Did he want an invitation to dine at his home? Every day he met new people, and he kept bumping into old friends from the province who had moved up in the ministry and were now influential in the capital. Simanovitsch knew how to take advantage of all this aid, and by the end of the third year in St. Petersburg he was seeing assurances of success.

As he was reading the morning paper one day in 1905, he spied a headline which chilled his heart: POGROM BREAKS IN KIEV. He was on the next train to Kiev. He had to pass his old shop, which he had left in the hands of a manager, on the way home from the station; he found it looted and burned and his friend murdered. Further on, as he passed by the synagogue, he saw a heap of bodies. They had been slain during the service and their corpses thrown out on the street. He recognized some of his relatives among the dead. When he finally reached home he uttered a prayer of thanksgiving to God that his family was unharmed. With the help of his local friends General Maurin and Chief of Police Zikotsky, he and his family hid from the crazed mobs until he was able to flee the country. His family still in Kiev, he ended up in Berlin, safe and sound, but with the indelible memory of the horror to haunt him. One can imagine the heat of these impressions, the agony of these recollections. It is a wonder that Simanovitsch did not become a bitter man. But he was sensitive without being spiteful, and he returned to his native land resolved in his heart to use all his hard-earned influence to ease the plight of Russian Jewry. A fighting man in best Hebraic style, Aaron Simanovitsch returned to St. Petersburg.

Fifteen miles to the south, the Imperial estate of Tsarskoye Selo, the residence of the Tsar of All the Russians, was a fairyland garden. But the lush lawns, bubbling streams, elegant drives, and softened woods were infested by the secret police. None of the dangers and exigencies of the outside world percolated through this screen of security, and the man who was Tsar and father of All the Russians presided over his Imperial household in an unreal environment. Into the making of this arena of palace and gardens had gone the experience and results of centuries of living under Imperial organization.

The House of Romanov had supplied Russia with her monarchs since the beginning of the reign of Michael Feodorovitch Romanov in 1613. In 1868, Maria Feodorovna, daughter-in-law of the Emperor Alexander II, gave birth to her first son, Nicholas. As first-born male offspring, he stood in line to inherit the crown upon his father's and grandfather's deaths.

His grandfather, Alexander II, had taken the risk and offered freedom to the serfs in the year 1861. The Tsar-Liberator, as he was later dubbed, was shot by a crazed revolutionary. This assassination embittered his son, who became Alexander III, a huge, dynamic, forceful, hard-working man who was grimly determined to restore the absoluteness of the autocracy and who set out on a crusade to crush the insurgent forces of liberation. His methods were adopted from ancient Sparta; he believed in the efficacy of a harsh, heavy discipline and saw to it that even his own family led regimented lives.

Nicholas' upbringing was entangled in all the myths and traditions which the monarchy had accumulated over its long history. His childhood days passed by under the ubiquitous and rigorous authority of his herculean father, Tsar Alexander III, whose wishes and theories ruled, planned, and divided the boy's young life into discreet compartments, so that Nicholas had to perform carefully ordered activities during specified times. Rituals and tutors surrounded him and dinned into his impressionable head the necessity of upholding the ancient Russian trinity of God, the Tsar, and the People. Here, in his tutors' chambers, he learned to live in the rich, psychic imagery of religion, to cherish the symbols of both Church and State, and to fear and hate those historic enemies of Russia, the Jews and the Poles.

His education proceeded apace according to his father's timetable. He never got the chance to steer his own course, to let himself drift languidly and indolently in the innocence of childhood. Completely oblivious to the passions which goaded Alexander III on, he grew up in awe of—and a little afraid of—his father's vitality. As Nicholas approached adulthood, he concerned himself only with the niceties of his existence: he cultivated the social arts, learned to be a sportsman, grew fond of pageantry and of parties. In short, Nicholas became a gentleman.

By 1894, Alexander III had succeeded in stabilizing the monarchy, which had been thrown askew during the previous reign, but he had destroyed his health in doing it. Life went out of him abruptly when he was forty-nine, and Nicholas, who hadn't counted on this, was quite unprepared to rule. For the past twenty-six years his life had been governed by an outside will and he had enjoyed the easiness of a life of irresponsibility. Now the casual, charming Nicky had become Nicholas II, Tsar of All the Russians. The reins of an empire devolved into his careless hands.

Nicholas responded to a new reality the only way he could, casually and amicably. He certainly looked the part. When he accepted the crown at his coronation, he cut a very handsome figure. If he took his short stature from his mother, he evidenced all his father's square, open-faced honesty. His mellow blue eyes excited one's sympathy at once. He stood in the sanctuary of the Cathedral in Moscow, resplendent in his red robes and carrying the golden crown on his smooth, auburn-haired head with all the air of a confident, mature emperor.

If one conducted any business with the young Tsar at one of his nightly receptions for this purpose, this image of confidence was likely to be enhanced by his fine, personable manner. He sat relaxed, attentive, and unpretentious in his elegant office. Affairs were conducted to the mutual satisfaction of all parties so easily that visitors were amazed. But pleasant surprise reverted to bitter disappointment later when one learned that the Tsar tended to leave his assurances suspended in the air in which they were spoken. Many times Nicholas simply forgot what he had promised. But many times, too, he simply avoided the steps it took to make his word good.

Nicholas' theories and opinions were a complex combination of superstition, science, and religion. He had been reared in an atmosphere heavy with the supernatural, and this respect for the mystic aspects of experience remained with him. Accordingly, superstition ran rampant in even the highest circles. In his court at any given time were a number of men who claimed kinship with the metaphysical world. These prophets and soothsayers were quite the vogue in turn-of-the-century Russia, exercising an influence upon all of its leading men and women. Countess Nina Sarnekova, the spiritualist, became the featured attraction at the famous banquets given by the Rumanian violinist Gulesco, who also enjoyed the close friendship of Nicholas II. It was not rare that these drinking banquets were interrupted by a summons from the Tsar, requesting their spiritualist-companionship at the palace. Frequently he called upon Nina to lead them into a seance from which he would gain a knowledge about his future. Among the members of this mysterious circle one found such men as Nicholas Nisharadze (a Caucasian prince), the Tsar's chamberlain; Ivan Nakashidze, the director of the Red Cross; Prince Utshad Dadiani, the adjutant of the Tsar; Prince Alexander Eristov; Prince Orbeliani, the Governor-General of Koutais; and other well-known members of society. It is small wonder that Rasputin was able to enjoy the fear and respect of Nicholas and his Court.

While the Tsar exhibited small concern for the intramural doings of his ministries, he displayed an avid interest in the relations of his Court. His greatest fears took root in the insecurity of the Crown.

The Dowager Empress Maria was a plump, gay, robust little woman of almost forty-seven when she was dethroned by the death of Alexander III and the accession of her son and daughter-in-law. In her position as figurehead of the Old Court—as this coterie of her old relations came to be called—she served as a gathering post for all the parties who were dissatisfied with Nicholas' presence on the throne. Maria herself had become comfortably accustomed to the splendid gaiety of life as the Tsarina, and this abrupt change in her life sat very poorly with her. She begrudged each and every surrender of rank and circumstance which was required of her demotion. For some weeks it was a question whether she would give up the crown jewels to Alexandra without an ugly fight. She disliked the very idea of her son being Tsar and forced him to consider the fearful possibility that she would prefer to enthrone one of his younger brothers, the Grand Duke George, and, later, the Grand Duke Michael. He considered it well within the capabilities of his mother and relatives, most of whom flocked to her side, to arrange for his deposition either by assassination or by palace revolution.

In 1903, when Nicholas received news of the assassination of King Alexander and Queen Draga of Serbia, he considered himself warned and filed away in his memory the image of a doomed monarch lying cold and bloody on the walk underneath his bedroom window. One can better understand why he shunned entanglement in petty ministerial contests when each day brought him new fears of palace intrigue.

As Rasputin was to tell Anastasia and Militsa on the day he first met them, normal men and women take their security in a full stomach, a plentiful storehouse, and a safe, warm home. The Tsar and Tsarina, who had palaces and guards, an Imperial income and Imperial provider, took their security from having provided the kingdom with an heir. Their greatest work was not in the fields, but in the bedchamber. Without a son to inherit the throne, the Romanov Dynasty had no future and was as ephemeral as it was magnificent.

Alexandra had proved her fertility four times; but each time she had brought forth a girl. Without a male child the Tsar had no heir and the future of the Crown lay enshrouded in doubt. In the past, the lack of an heir had been a sufficient reason to call for a Tsar's abdication, and when his fourth daughter was born, Nicholas began to worry.

The brazen men and women in his court ridiculed this preponderance of female siblings—the Grand Duchesses Olga, Tatiana, Maria, and Anastasia—and challenged the Tsar's virility. These opinions reached Nicholas, and he took them seriously. When he sought the advice of the present crop of soothsayers at Court, they responded in a similar manner. "It is your fault," they said. "You shall never sire a male. It is not in you to do it." So Nicholas let himself be convinced of his inability to bring forth an heir and grew despondent.

Rumors and gossip were the fare of social intercourse at the

Tsar's court. Only reluctantly would Nicholas II face the situation: he could either temporarily renounce his marriage claims on his wife, or face the impending struggle with his family without the prospect of an heir. He decided that the latter involved too much risk, and so—according to rumors—he chose to give over his conjugal relationship with Alexandra to another man.

Of course, this expedient was said to have been adopted behind the protective shield of the army and secret police. No one outside of Nicholas, Alexandra, and the man in question knew of this arrangement—no one, that is, other than the omniscient Rasputin, who was informed later. Nicholas' choice of surrogate was not hard to make: Alexandra had been friendly with a certain individual for over a year now. Her intimacy with him was just the natural end of a natural development of mutual affection. He was the dashing, mustachioed commander of the Uhlan Regiment of the Empress Alexandra, General Alexander Orlov.

As far as the public was concerned, Alexandra's fifth pregnancy proceeded normally; no one even suspected that Nicholas was not the father. But as her time drew near both Alexandra and Nicholas grew anxious. The delivery was abnormal. The infant appeared in the worst possible presentation: shoulder first. When the attending physicians informed Nicholas of the necessity of an operation and asked him for instructions, he replied, "If the child is a male, do what is necessary to save him—spare no means whatsoever. If the child is a girl, put the mother's life first. If it is a son, you must save it, you must. Go, and bring me word immediately."

The child was a boy, but the doctors were able to save both mother and infant. The birth of an heir brought so much relief to Nicholas that he did not even mind the doctor's telling him that his wife could never again conceive; the operation had demanded the removal of her uterus and ovaries. For Alexandra, too, the birth brought relief—but from the ladies of the Court she heard the gist of Nicholas' speech to the doctors. A cold spot formed on her heart and she never again felt comfortable or certain about her husband.

Alexandra's fifth child and only son was named Alexis after Nicholas' familial hero, the seventeenth-century tsar of that name.

Her chagrin over her husband's expression of disloyalty was said to have made her relationship with General Orlov all the more important to her. Nicholas was no longer the center of feeling in her life. The distance between them grew, and she confided in Orlov more and more. Finally, as rumor had it, the Tsarina fell hopelessly in love with him, and Nicholas had lost her forever.

The lovers could not long conceal their vigorous affection from the gaze of the public. A scandal was brewing whose proportions might very well have engulfed Nicholas in disaster. To avert its breaking, the Tsar decided to take the only action available to him: he ordered Orlov to prepare to assume the command of his regiments in Egypt. Before Orlov's departure Nicholas invited the general to dine with him privately at the palace—a sort of gentlemanly *bon voyage.* The general was carried home from this dinner party unconscious on a stretcher. He died on the train to Istanbul.

Nicholas feigned shock and grief. He had the general's body entombed with great martial ceremony in a grassy knoll on the grounds of Tsarskoye Selo. Alexandra could often be seen arranging flowers on the grave, mingling their fragrance and softness with her tears. Her relationship with Nicholas never healed, as grief and bitterness overcame her. Heartbroken, she gave herself up to despair and was the frequent victim of hysterical fits.

Nicholas respected his wife's grief and remained aloof for many weeks. Even when he did attempt to restore their relations— verbally—he didn't approach her in person. He sent Fleet Lieutenant Chagin, the well-loved master of their yacht, the *Standart,* to prepare his way. In this delicate manner, they began once again to speak to each other, and a semblance of domestic harmony returned to the Imperial Family.

But these optimistic chords sounded only briefly. A nurse noticed a queer-looking bruise on the year-old infant's pudgy leg. It had no apparent cause. The child was well-attended and wasn't spry enough to have climbed out of his crib and inflicted it on himself. Doctors were called in to investigate.

Once again, Fate had dealt Nicholas and his family a heavy blow. Alexis had been born into this world afflicted with hemophilia, and none of the advantages of the Imperial estate could lessen the horror of this boy's life. The slightest break in the smallest vessels of his body set into motion a hellish chain of events. Where a normal boy received a bruise, Alexis received a trauma. His blood would flow out of his vessels and into the skin, and nothing would stop this seepage until the cavity was filled with blood and the pressure of the swollen tissue sealed off the break. This process could take days, and during it all the boy would experience excruciating agony.

All of the best physicians of the realm tried their hand at the impossible cure and all the charlatans and holy men offered their vacant advice. But the Tsar and Tsarina continued to hope that a cure could be found.

But it was not Fate alone which brought Alexis to his severest trial in his fifth year. He was playing with his chamberlain in the palace garden. At a little distance, two gardeners were engaged in pruning the profusion of bushes and hedges which surrounded the palace. Suddenly, one of them pulled out a knife and hurled it at Alexis. The blade found its way into the thigh of the boy. The horrified chamberlain leaped upon the nearest gardener, strangled him purple, and killed him right on the spot. Doctors rushed to the scene and applied the necessary bandages and carried the boy to his bedroom. The guards apprehended the fleeing second gardener as he approached the gate and brought him to Nicholas.

Nicholas immediately interrogated the captive. He learned that the man and his partner had formerly been in the service of the *Standart*, his yacht; before that they had been gardeners at the Anichkov Palace. When two places had recently opened in the gardening service at Tsarskoye Selo, they had been preferred by Chagin, the master of the yacht, acting on the request of some of Nicholas' relatives, but with no idea of their purposes.

After receiving this information, Nicholas immediately ordered the prisoner to be shot and sent for Chagin. When Chagin learned what had transpired and heard the part he had unwittingly played, he wrote a hasty letter of apology to the Tsar, went outside, put a rifle in his mouth, and blew off his head.

This ended the investigation, for Nicholas was too frightened of his uncles and cousins to confront them with such meager evidence. He would let the matter rest and double his vigilance over his son.

The wound took weeks to heal and caused Alexis untold pain, instilling in him an unnatural mistrust of any and all outsiders. He was bedridden for months.

After these harrowing events Tsar Nicholas II began exercising the ancient birthright of Russian males, and was more and more often to be seen drunk. The domestic bone of contention—the proper way to treat the stricken Tsarevitch Alexis—had been chewed upon with much rigor recently. The ferocity of the Imperial quarrels was manifest in the silences which passed between Alexandra and Nicholas for as long as a week at a time. To these pressures was added the heat of the smoldering domestic discontent and the horror and embarrassment of the war with Japan of 1904–5. The Tsar's vaunted military forces had been cut to ribbons in short order by the alleged Japanese "monkeys" in the Russo-Japanese War.

Alexandra lapsed into a quiet, eerie silence and refused to withdraw from the Tsarevitch's side, even to sleep. Her life became an agony of self-incrimination and grief over the child's sufferings, because she blamed herself for passing the disease on to her son. She withdrew from contact with the outside world and remained unconsoled and despairing until the appearance of Rasputin brought hope into both her and the boy's lives.

THREE

Aaron Simanovitsch was a vital man with a great need for excitement, and this need took him to the racetracks during the day and to the St. Petersburg nightclubs and music halls, to the banquets and imperial balls in the evenings. He mingled his name and his money with the best of the empire and one could often discover his handsome figure at the table where fortunes changed hands in the flip of a card.

It is well known that the rich have a penchant for gambling and a love for the sport of Fate. Imperial Russia at the turn of the century was no exception to this generalization. Simanovitsch's own passion for gambling was voracious and the stakes he risked enormous. It is said that a Rothschild once owed him six million dollars at the end of a night. And so, through this brotherhood of gamblers, he gained access to a very high society and his circle of friends grew steadily closer to the mainspring of all social and political life in Russia, the Imperial Family.

As he turned each contact into acquaintance and each acquaintance into friendship, Simanovitsch became increasingly aware of the private goings-on at the Court. He searched out the details and gradually became familiar with its daily life. One evening, in a nightspot in St. Petersburg, his tentative investigations were rewarded. One of the Princes Wittgenstein, an officer in the palace guard, had been riding the crest of an incredible wave of gambler's luck; he had backed down all comers, even the house. The room was crowded, smoky, tense, and quiet at the pinnacle of this achievement. The house had just refused the bank. The Prince stared hard, anger making a flush on his gaunt cheeks; it was four o'clock in the morning and the Prince didn't want to stop. Aaron Simanovitsch quietly uttered the word, "Banco," and took his place opposite the Prince. In four hours he had cut the Prince's winnings of a week in half—and in the ensuing early morning orgy, he and the Prince became fast friends.

Soon Prince Wittgenstein realized the great value of a friendship with Simanovitsch. Neither he nor his brother—nor, indeed, any member of the Court—had any command of economic reality. Aaron Simanovitsch not only knew the rules of mercantile sport, but he was willing to act on behalf of his aristocratic friends. Of course, he would look into this confusing little matter of finances, this little matter of gambling debts and of credit, which troubled the Prince. Most likely, he resolved it with a handsome profit.

The news of Simanovitsch's acumen spread rapidly. Not long after his fateful meeting with the Prince, he was presented to the Princess Orbeliani, rumored to be the former mistress of the Tsar. He returned often to her house that season, where he met the ladies-in-waiting of the Empress Alexandra, the officers of the guard, the Caucasian Nobles, Prince Utshad Dadiani, Prince Alexander Amilakhvari, and many of the people who served in the palace and were influential at Court, including Poincée, the *maître d'hôtel* of the Palace. He extended his charm and his services to all. Together with one of the Princes, he even set up a court chess club which was nothing other than a front for gambling. Simanovitsch's passion for gambling made him all the more at home in the Imperial Court and extended his influence even to the friends of the Tsar.

For some reason, perhaps his natural cautiousness, Simanovitsch waited until he was established at the house of Princess Orbeliani to let it be known that he was a jeweler by profession. But when he did, he fast became indispensable to the Court ladies. Here, aiding these good women through the most tender and secret money transactions, he gained the trust and good wishes of many highly placed persons. He grew to be an important man in the realm, with important friends who regarded his wishes. His confidence grew, and he was established at last.

Finally, to complete his triumph, he met the Tsarina, the Empress Alexandra. Impressed by Simanovitsch, she invited him to the palace to look at her jewels—a great honor, for the crown jewels comprised one of the few passions of the Empress and were in themselves a fortune worth countless millions. Alexandra bestowed commissions on Simanovitsch to purchase gems for her, and he carried them out swiftly and conscientiously. Knowing her thriftiness, he sold her his gems at a ruinously low price. Even the court jeweler, the world-renowned Peter Carl Fabergé, was amazed when he discovered how little the Tsarina Alexandra had paid for the gems. But what did this financial loss matter to Simanovitsch? He gained the trust and confidence of the Empress of All the Russians. She continued to ask him to do favors for her. He let her buy on installment, gave bargains to her friends, and thus became friends with them too.

But if this last year of 1915 gave unqualified success to Aaron Simanovitsch, it had brought nothing but troubles to the Imperial couple. The economy was in great disturbance; there was discontent in the realm and uncertainty throughout the country. And thanks to Nicholas II's mystical sympathies, the Court was crowded with a constant stream of monks, prophets, priests, and charlatans who offered their panaceas and left when they failed. Even the simplest questions of life drew out the most capricious theories, for there were no great institutions of science or knowledge such as dictated the truth to our Western nations. Mystery penetrated into all areas of life, with the Orthodox Church holding sway over the millions of peasants and providing the answers such as they believed them to be. Religion provided the means to escape despair and live forthrightly in a miserable universe. Its doctrines and teachings anesthetized the pain of the poor and gave the rich an apology for their wealth and a chance for recreation. Russian folklore was flooded with the fame of the monasteries and saints, and pilgrimages to the holy places were frequently made by people from all levels of society. The Grand Duchesses Anastasia and Militsa, the wives of the cousins of the Tsar, the Grand Dukes Nicholas and Peter, found at the end of a two-year pilgrimage a source of succor for the tribulations of the Imperial Family.

They had been traveling all about the western portions of Russia on their way to Jerusalem. One morning, as they were nearing a copse of pines on their morning perambulation about the grounds of the monastery of Saint Michael, they encountered a man dressed in the customary habit of the *moujik*, the Russian peasant. He was chopping wood, his blouse soaked with the perspiration of his effort, and the genteel ladies were drawn to this novel sight.

"Why do you chop this wood, peasant?" they questioned him.

"It is my livelihood," said the man. "I chop wood so that I can eat. I was not born a duke, so I must chop."

There was something about his forthright manner which captivated them. They were excited by him and kept up the conversation. They asked him more questions: "How long have you worked here?" "Where do you come from?" "What have you done before this?" "Where have you been before this? Have you traveled?"

The man, Grigori Yefimovich Rasputin, whose last name means in Russian "the Dissolute," answered all their questions courteously and fully. He told them that he was a simple man from the village of Pokrovskoye in the district of Tobolsk. His family consisted of his father, who worked loading and unloading barges on the river Tura, his wife Praskovia, and his daughters, Maria and Varia, who lived with him and his wife in the village. He told them that he was uneducated and that he could scarcely read, but that he nevertheless possessed the Word of God, which he preached to the people on railroads and on the platforms in the stations and on steamboat landings. He boasted the power of this preaching and even wagered that he could defeat a well-schooled missionary or cleric on this holy battleground. He alluded to his travels, his pilgrimages, his great sufferings. He completely captivated Anastasia and Militsa who had become bored with their imperial retinue, and they invited him to take tea with them that very afternoon.

When he entered their apartments at the monastery, Rasputin became aware of the great wealth of these ladies. He took the greatest pains to please them, recounting the tales of his pilgrimages and how he had walked from Tobolsk to Jerusalem and back, and regaling them with what he saw and what he did. He returned many times to their rooms and discoursed at great length and with great eloquence on his impressions of all the famous monasteries he had seen and all the famous holy men he had met. He soon became a regular figure in the salons of these great ladies of St. Petersburg.

The letters which arrived at the homes of their friends at the capital were filled with the news and excitement of their find. Princess Orbeliani and Anna Vyrubova were two who were especially close to the Imperial couple. Anna, in fact, was the closest friend and confidante of the Tsarina. When she heard about Rasputin, she couldn't contain her emotion. She knew of the malaise at Tsarskoye Selo, the winter residence of the Court, having experienced the strain of their grief at first hand. She spoke to Alexandra concerning this strange man, telling her of his famed holiness and simplicity, of his reputation as a healer, and of his knowledge of sacred law and the Scriptures. She told the Empress that Rasputin could prophesy the future, ward off misfortune, and use his esoteric knowledge of herbs and plants to cure disease.

The Tsar sent for Rasputin.

Anastasia received word of the Imperial wish with joy in her heart. For wasn't Rasputin hers? Hadn't she been the instrument of his sudden recognition? She, of course, felt herself responsible for the safe and swift conveyance of Rasputin to the Tsar, and she had hatched magnificent plans for the execution of her responsibility. She had the way from Pokrovskoye to St. Petersburg filled with all the carriages, coaches, trains, and ferries the Imperial retinue would need to make their way. Anastasia planned on being Rasputin's escort and may have dreamed during restless nights of the more intimate services and tasks this self-imposed dedication would require her to perform. However, on the morning Rasputin arrived in St. Petersburg, as another in a long series of possible healers, Anastasia was not with him and her plan to be his escort did not materialize.

Apparently Rasputin rejected at least the more material favors proferred by the early devotee. Uninterested in display, he elected to enter the capital in the garb of a *moujik*. It was not a gleaming carriage which carried this man into the great city; he went on his own naked feet. A man of the people, not a spaniel of the rich, he didn't want to surround himself with the florid accoutrements of wealth and power.

This attitude did not derive from abstract formulae and logical sequences. Rasputin was no academician; he tittered at the thought of mathematics. Neither was he a politician, setting down success to a ratio of chances and defining victory as the perfection of a plan. Rasputin's knowledge was the wisdom of the sensual man, of the man born into the world of flesh and blood, a world of sky and forest, of mountain and river. The blue sky was also the sender of biting, winter snows; the ancient green forest battered muscle and sinew in the race to gather fuel for the winter; the mountain could disgorge an avalanche of either earth or snow, and spring rivers could burst with watery excess. To stay alive a man had to be more cunning than the elements. Some call this knowledge intuition or instinct—and feel secure for a mystery has been pigeonholed—but Rasputin knew it to be the understanding of the animal, the wordless thoughts of the beast.

Thus Rasputin acted with the immediacy of desire. He felt the pebbles and gravel under his feet and the dust in his toes as he entered St. Petersburg that morning, and he went straight to the monastery where Theophan presided over the Theological Academy. His reputation had preceded him and had culled from this great bishop an invitation for Rasputin to spend here his first days in the capital. He accepted the offer out of a desire to display the religious threads in the complex tapestry of his personality and to confront this aged and reverend prelate with the fervor of his own faith, the wisdom of his own soul, and the pure authority which emanated from his person.

During the first months of his stay, he was to meet all the great figures in the hierarchy of the Orthodox Church. To all Rasputin extended his mirth and good fellowship. To each alike he offered his robust good humor and his steely certitude in the Will of the Almighty. Rasputin's presence flashed before the weary eyes of these bent men, who had been attempting to cement the great cracks and fissures in the brittle empire, as a sign from Heaven that he had been "sent" to do the Lord's work. They hailed him as a genuine holy man and raised prayers of joy and thanksgiving to their Creator's infinite wisdom.

FOUR

The Grand Duchess Anastasia, fulfilling her dreams, met Rasputin in St. Petersburg and took him to his first Court appearance. He came marked as a *moujik* in a loose-fitting, coarse blouse and baggy old pants that ended inside muddied leather boots. He came in full knowledge of the august nature of his reviewers and acted with the serenity and reservation of a holy peasant. He didn't boast of his powers or display his sagacity; he neither made jokes nor laughed. No, Rasputin knew that he was at the palace of the Emperor and Empress of Russia, in the bedroom of an ailing heir. The intimacy and urgency of the Imperial Family's great need called for Rasputin's vast reservoirs of tranquility and certitude, with which he completely quenched anxiety. His effect as he stood at the foot of the bed bowed in prayer was like the effect of that great teacher long ago who spoke to the Galilean winds and sea. For the first time in an eight-year nightmare, peace had come to the Imperial Family.

The intimacy of this scene was well protected behind the screen of security surrounding the palace. No one outside the immediate family even knew the nature of Alexis' illness; thus, none knew the nature of Rasputin's favor. Why was this rough peasant a frequent visitor at the Court? What was his relation to the Tsar? What power did he exert over the Tsar that resulted in these repeated calls to the palace? What were Anastasia and Anna Vyrubova up to when they spoke to the Tsar in Rasputin's favor? Was it a design of the German Kaiser to defeat the House of Romanov?

As is the case with most conspiratorial theories, this one contained no truth: Anastasia was a loyal cousin of the Tsar, and Anna Vyrubova was still the friend and confidante of the poor Empress; they wished only to serve the Imperial house by bringing in a miracle worker. But as long as the Tsarevitch's illness was shrouded in secrecy, the relation of Rasputin to the Imperial Family was the subject of rumor.

These rumors made it impossible for Rasputin to live at Tsarskoye Selo, and so he remained in St. Petersburg where he could be seen. He stayed at the monastery only briefly before moving to the home of General Lotshtin on Nikolai Street. The general's wife was ever devoted to this gruff peasant—as were many genteel ladies—and hoped to win his favor by teaching him how to read. But he grew tired of her prattling and moved in with a relative of the Minister of Foreign Affairs, Mr. Sazonov of Yamskaya Street. Later on he would move in with the Englishman Cavett, and still later he ended his days in his own apartments at 64 Gorokhovaya Street.

The Tsar's irresponsible style was still making many enemies out of injured supporters. The Tsar showed small concern for this, however, and continued to perform his duties to the public in a rather perfunctory manner. One day Rasputin brought him up on this point, and the Tsar made a very revealing reply:

"Rasputin, you find fault with me for ignoring Mrs. Verblin's claims for her husband. But don't you know Mr. N——— of the ——— Ministry? How shall I deal with him, eh? I do not trust him more than to say hello. If I should go to him with this claim he should say, 'Certainly, Your Majesty, I will be most pleased to look into this matter of Mr. Verblin's promotion.' And he would smile so lavishly and we would sip some of his precious sherry and that would end the case of Mr. Verblin's claim. Eh? Why should I bother? It would just give him a chance to come later and bother me with some one of his interminable schemes."

"But Your Majesty," Rasputin replied, "if you do not trust him to do your bidding, then get another man to be the Tsar's minister. That is your prerogative."

"Nonsense," the Tsar shot back. "If I did that, what ministers would I have left? Who is it that I can trust? Whose fingers are clean and pure? For me, I do not trust anyone over three years old. When a boy reaches three, he learns to lie to please his elders. It is the end of innocence. No, my friend, they are all the same. It would do no good to change ministers."

This cynical attitude sapped Nicholas of the energy of good faith which fuels the most ordinary accomplishments. He left these inner affairs of government to sift out for themselves and to be accomplished by those who had the stomach for them. In such a situation Rasputin was able to exercise great power; he directed many of these enterprises by taking advantage of Nicholas' reluctance to carry them through.

In 1905, pressed to the limit by the defeats in the war with Japan and the imminent political upheaval, Nicholas was forced to accede to the revolutionary forces and grant a constitution. Though the document spoke weakly and offered but nominal powers to the newly created congress, the *Duma*, Nicholas' Imperial relatives were furious, and there were numerous subtle "hints" that he would endanger his position by going through with the move. But he did go through with the reforms, even though it caused such a family row that his advisers urged him to administer a second oath of loyalty to his relatives to ensure their support of the new government—or at least to put this support on some kind of record in case they tried anything later. Rasputin especially urged Nicholas to take strong actions against his family, showing the Emperor that it was an unequivocal situation which required an equally simple, clear-cut and forceful strategy.

But the Tsar remained loathe to take the offensive against his blood relations; the idea of such offensive moves against his family was repugnant to his gentlemanly sensibilities. He preferred the less obtrusive method of self-defense. It was to this end that he spent his energies building up an efficient bodyguard.

He needed a band of men whom he could trust implicitly, and he handpicked them from the ranks of the Tatar and Georgian regiments of southern Russia—fierce, swarthy soldiers who needed but a cause and a leader to make them invincible. Nicholas knew much depended on the qualities of the man he chose to lead this palace contingent, and he searched the ranks of the officers until he found his man in the person of Utshad Dadiani, a fiery Caucasian prince who readily dedicated his life to the safekeeping of the Tsar and his family: "I shall be most honored to place my life at the service of the Russian Tsar, Your Majesty. I give it over to you to do what you will with it whenever you desire. I place myself in your service fully and with no conditions attached, with the deepest sense of honor and pride in the undertaking."

Though their red and gold uniforms set them apart from the rest of the palace regiments, Nicholas' personal guard could be recognized by other criteria also. This passionate elite corps set a high value on their reputation as a bunch of debauchees. Their sexual escapades and unequaled drinking bouts earned them widespread fame in both military and civilian circles. Gulesco, the violinist, won Nicholas' undying friendship when he composed a merry song dealing with the soldiers of the Tsar's guard who had forgotten to pay the bill of an evenings' sport in a house of pleasure. The song ended in the refrain: "Give me my three rubles!" and was heard in many a drinking bar in St. Petersburg that season.

Nicholas viewed these trivial scandals with an amused eye. He knew each one of these men would lay down his life on the spot for any member of his family and would immediately draw his pistol and shoot to kill anyone the Tsar told him to. He could tolerate their fiery temperament—indeed, perhaps one day his life would depend on the passion of their dedication to him. So Nicholas continued to smile at their excesses and even helped them out of gambling debts and similar inconveniences whenever he could. These little services became an unspoken condition of the arrangement between the Tsar and his guard.

Rasputin had three principal haunts: the mansions of the rich, his own dining room, and the nightclubs and music halls of St. Petersburg. His style of partying was loose, fiery, and exhausting, for he possessed the charisma to send a celebration into unheard-of heights of vivacity. He had no fortune and no title, but his life became the prototype for a host of riotous followers. He inspired legions of young nobles to launch hot, unholy careers as rakes and thus he accumulated a most motley set of votaries.

On the road leading up to the Tsar's residence at Tsarskoye Selo, many noblemen had constructed stately mansions to serve as the centers of social intercourse during the winter season. Great parties competed with each other across the way, flowed into the dawn and early morning, softened for the glare of noon, and picked up again the next evening down the road a bit, at another house.

These affairs attracted men and women from all over civilized Russia and gave them a chance to dress up in their silk and lace finery, to display and covet veritable mountains of jewelry, and to ride in their magnificent carriages and exercise their great horses. Legions of musicians played in the mobile orchestras which produced the grand waltzes, the quadrilles, and the mazurkas for their dances. Lengths and lengths of tables were arrayed with the succulent cuisine of the aristocrats' kitchens. Wines and liquors from around the world flowed down their noble throats, making them hot and flushed in the general glow. A silly quarrel might very easily end in a duel at dawn. The guns would crack in the air over the dewy lawn and a young, resplendent officer might fall to the ground, staining the green grass with his blood. It was a time for gaudy ostentation and gallantry—a pretty and wasteful hysteria.

Rasputin hated these men, with all their costly forms and fashions, their superficial pleasantries and back-stabbing slanders. He thought them weak, ridiculous fops and he took it upon himself to insult them whenever occasion allowed. .

Yet for all his loathing of these decadent social circles, Rasputin became a frequent figure in the homes of both the rich and the royal. Sheltered by the umbrella of Imperial favor, he attended their parties, drank their wines, devoured their sweetmeats and delicacies and took their women with impunity. This last activity earned him the bitterness and hatred of many wronged men, from generals to court fops. But since he took all his cues from his appetites, living for the day, his enemies' complaints didn't bother him in the least.

Anyone who attended one of these parties would have had no problem in recognizing Rasputin. In the middle of an elegant salon, lighted by the flames of a thousand candles in crystal candelabras, and fragrant with the perfume of numerous infatuated women, stood a peasant. His stature conformed to the stocky, full-necked proportions of an average *moujik*. His hair fell down in a brown oily tangle to his shoulders and was complemented by a reddish-brown beard that flared out from his high-boned cheeks. If you watched him closely during the night, you would see him arranging his hair very carefully over the left portion of his broad forehead. He had a bump there which his vanity demanded he disguise beneath his thick bangs. His clothing was the standard *moujik* costume, except that his shirt was silk and his boots polished.

The Villa Rodé, a popular nightclub in town, paid high homage to the consistency and quality of Rasputin's social life when its manager decided to construct a separate wing to house the feasting of this peasant and his clan. Rasputin stocked these get-togethers with leading characters from the social register and spiced them with additions from the ranks of the professionals. Professional women, mistresses, actresses, and all the kept women of official St. Petersburg were called on to add to the general revelry. Interspersed among this band of flirting women were generals who had favors to ask, candidates for ministerial and other posts, officers and officials of the Imperial establishment, and, of course, the young rakes. Rasputin, host and leader, would arrive at night with his pockets stuffed with all sorts of colorful baubles and trinkets. He had bright green silk scarves and yellow handkerchiefs, pungent perfumes and tasty candies. He had a gypsy-choir imported from Poland to make the fierce melodies which would set his soul in motion. He danced in his heavy boots as only the Russian peasant knows how and passed out his prizes to the women who caught his fancy, yelling, "Gypsy girls have robbed me! Dance, dance, dance for your souls!"

His eyes were gray and lustrous, and those he pinned in his gaze found it a hard task to turn away. His presence emanated from those gray orbs, filled the room, and claimed the time and place as his. The intensity of his gaze became notorious and feared.

One night as he leaped onto the dance floor and turned, looking to choose a dancing partner, several young officers unsheathed their swords and several young men drew pistols which they had concealed. This stunned everyone into a momentary silence. Then Rasputin turned his fiery gaze upon the young conspirators and shouted out: "You want to kill me!"

They were stricken by the shame of their desires and their resolve wavered under the authority of Rasputin's piercing eyes, so intensely vibrant before them. The whole company was struck dumb and, except for the wind at the windows and the fire on the crackling logs, there was not a sound. In a quiet, calm voice, Rasputin said, "You were my enemies once. Now you are my enemies no more. You have seen that my soul can conquer. Go. Do not return again, but hasten home. You can never master me—I have power over you forever because of the evil of your deed. Leave us quickly."

The young officers were utterly defeated. They repented at once, to the very depths of their souls. "Forgive us!" they cried, begging Rasputin to reconsider, falling to their knees to beg forgiveness.

Rasputin softened, but he knew their hearts and wished to make examples of them. "I will never forgive you," he said, "for I have not invited you here. I was not glad when I saw you arrive; and I shall not be sad to see you leave. Begone. Now! You are healed. Your evil wishes are turned aside. Let me remain here with my own and amuse myself. Depart."

They left, and the party continued.

The bedroom to which he eventually brought his conquests was located in the apartments at 64 Gorokhovaya. Not surprisingly, his was a modest domicile. His bedroom was of no great size, with paper on the walls, a bare wooden floor, and a great brick fireplace to ward off the freezing winter cold. It contained only three pieces of furniture: a small wooden table, a hard-backed chair, and a great stained-wood double bed with a hard horsehair mattress and a great woolen quilt. A window facing west allowed the yellow-orange rays of the Russian sun to slant onto the bedstead in the afternoon and let in the moonlight at night and the glitter of a low star or two.

One might wonder at the modesty of Rasputin's domestic arrangements. But Rasputin was rich in passions, not notions. He spent his energies living, not scheming; he gave no consideration to such matters as wealth and rank, except, of course, with regard to the Tsar himself, whom he revered with the Russian peasant's tenacity. Only in his workroom did Rasputin allow himself touches of elegance, and these were mere daubs of it—two great leather chairs. The rest of his house—the dining room, the kitchen, the halls, and the foyer—were all of the same bare wooden simplicity as his bedroom. And because the humble side of Rasputin's personality would countenance no servants, so his household served itself.

There was, however, another room in which his daughters Maria and Varia lived, to whom he was generous and devoted. He decorated their room with a surprising elegance. Their furniture was upholstered in the warmth of red and the luster of silk. Their floor shone with the luminous depth of polished mahogany, and their walls were softened with rare tapestry. They did well by him, and he sheltered them from both the turbulence of his own passions and the hatred of his vociferous enemies. Not that they were lonely, for their room communicated with the kitchen and the room where their two cousins, Nijura and Katia, lived.

Maria and Varia believed their father was a good man who led a hard life burdened with the heavy responsibility of rule. They revered him, as all good daughters revere a hard-working conscientious papa.

Had Rasputin converted his hedonistic drives into avarice, as so many unfortunate successes do, he would have rivaled the Tsar himself in material possessions. For what kind of prices befitted the favors he dealt out? Wasn't the head of state worth an estate or two? Couldn't he have bartered a government contract of millions for a Siberian gold mine or two? Untold wealth was his for the asking, but he didn't ask. He preferred sensuous to acquisitive pleasures, the pulse of life to the glitter of gold.

But even living in the cradle of one's senses as Rasputin did, one must still have someone to attend to the needs of the future and the debts of the past. At the house of Princess Orbeliani Rasputin met his man—Aaron Simanovitsch.

Anna Vyrubova was the instrument of this meeting; she had been worried about the financial underpinnings of Rasputin's career. Indeed, what was his income but the sporadic alms of the Tsar? Vyrubova knew where to go for help in these matters and thus introduced Rasputin to Simanovitsch at one of the Princess' parties.

Rasputin was eager to talk to Simanovitsch, who in turn was only too glad to talk to Rasputin. The peasant admitted his financial illiteracy and plied the jeweler with a hundred questions; Simanovitsch recited the commercial canon and displayed his knowledge

of the various and myriad relations of the courtiers. In this way, a
friendship was joined which eventually developed into something of
a partnership: Simanovitsch assumed the functions of secretary,
administrator, adviser, and confidant in Rasputin's life, and Rasputin
conferred with Simanovitsch before making any decisions. As this
relationship became indispensable to Rasputin, Aaron Simanovitsch's influence penetrated, at last, to the throne itself.

FIVE

As Rasputin's confidant, Aaron Simanovitsch had an opportunity to witness the intimate but nonetheless complex side of the Dissolute One's personality. Rasputin's wife came to town once a year from her village of Pokrovskoye, in western Siberia, across the Ural Mountains, to visit papa and his daughters. She came joyously and modestly for she had the Russian peasant woman's native respect for the privacy and freedom of her husband's life. In turn, when the Tsar called him, Rasputin gave Praskovia her freedom. If she chose not to relinquish her communion with the lush Siberian land, then that was her prerogative; he would not interfere. Her visits were occasions to celebrate, not reasons to quarrel. Rasputin submitted to her when she visited at the spring of each year. She would keep her visits short and unobtrusive. She knew the way he lived: he was no different than when he was back home making love to all the village girls. He would always be profligate, and she would always understand. He would act freely in her presence and kiss a lady on the cheek to show that he thought Praskovia was as good as the nobility. They had a merry time together and parted best of friends; they remained man and wife until her death.

Rasputin and his wife Praskovia also had a son, Dimitri. The poor boy, a quiet fellow, was slightly in awe of his father. He was the kind of sweet-faced child who walked around in his own private little world, who was more kind than intelligent, and who grew up into a quiet, sturdy man, content to live coolly in the shade of his father's greatness. At the bequest of his father, Dimitri attempted to pass some studies at the Theological Academy. But it was a hopeless task; his mind just would not take to the small characters of the printed page. So after two years of failing efforts and shame at his own incompetence, Dimitri broke with his father's hopes for him and left St. Petersburg for the land of his mother. He bought a farm with the help of Rasputin with whom he had parted in friendship and planted himself in the good earth to toil as he could. When the war arrived, his father did not forget him. Rasputin's concern for Dimitri's safety crossed over the mountains and placed at his son's cottage door an order to appear ready for service—in the Imperial Sanitation Department. If there were several windows into Rasputin's soul, this one shows a glimpse of his humanity.

When Rasputin wasn't out on the town or at another's party, he entertained at home. His dinners formally took place between ten and one but usually lasted well into the early morning. His guests always gathered in the dining room, the largest room in the house, and sometimes as many as two hundred crowded in to enjoy the festivities.

The room was longer than it was wide, and it stretched from the east to the west side of the house. In each end wall were three great curtained windows that let in the morning sun and the sunset. A huge arched stone hearth stood in the center of one of the long walls. Rasputin himself arranged the five-foot logs before each dinner. The leaping flames and popping sparks reminded him of his years in the vast evergreen forests of Siberia.

One entered the room through the doorway which faced the hearth across the room. To the right and to the left of the doors, long wooden sideboards and cupboards lined the wall, containing the pots, pans, utensils, cutlery, and crockery of Rasputin's household. On the sideboards rested the large platters and big wooden bowls filled with the fish, fruit, bread, and vegetables brought by Simanovitsch and many of the guests. The only furniture in the room was a long oaken banquet table and the straight-backed chairs and simple benches which lined it. The table had no cloth, not even cotton: Rasputin liked the bare wood.

These banquets often bordered on the macabre. Generals, high officers in the Imperial Guard, gallant rakes, princesses, court ladies, ballerinas, actresses, and ranking mistresses threw in their lot together with supplementary peasants, urgent, frightened Jews, vagrants, paupers, and beggars—all with the united purpose of currying the magic favor of one they unanimously regarded as a boor.

Rasputin had a great opinion of the value of his own words, but only a slight opinion of the value of his audience. His manner was as crude as it was laconic. He spoke softly, often muttering; one had to pay close attention to understand what he said. His clean, hard body drew out the passions of these laced-up women; he insulted them, gibed at them, made obscene gestures and gross allusions. But still he magnetized them; they came figuratively to lick his boots. To them he was holy. They flocked to him to offer themselves up body and soul, and he chose from among them. They loved his earthiness, his holiness, his mystic ambiance, and his brusqueness. A night in bed with him seemed to purge their souls and clean their impure bodies; his crude treatment satisfied their guilty consciences and left them with a true mystic experience.

Some of these great ladies came to him swollen with importance and taken with the rustle and glitter of their own elegant attire. They expected Rasputin to accept them gladly, as prized trophies. But he would not tolerate their haughtiness. If they were lucky, he simply ignored them; if not, he would heap abuse upon these confused, embarrassed ladies in the most graphic and vernacular argot. Even their liverymen learned new things from his vile mouth.

Rasputin felt at his best when poised over the naive, light, frightened creatures who came to him with soleful, ignorant eyes. But the ladies who fired Rasputin to his very core were the reluctant ones who abhorred his touch. He would taunt them and exhort them, insult them and flatter them, sometimes even crossing over the line separating civilized from barbaric play. He wasn't above blackmail and could easily make or break a career with the utterance of one word.

Whether or not his heart reached out in compassion and warmth, Rasputin's manners were nothing less than atrocious. They grew almost evil in their nature because Rasputin consciously fashioned a peculiar, disgusting ritual out of them. Fish soup is an ancient

Russian staple, and Rasputin always had a big steaming pot of it on hand, together with hunks of coarse black bread. He used to tear off a piece of bread, sprinkle a layer of salt on it, and then dunk his hand up to his knuckles into the bowl of soup. When the bread was saturated, he extracted it and sucked off a bit, slurping it noisily through the black stumps which were all that remained of his teeth. Soup would dribble down and catch in his beard and roll down his hands and wrists onto his shirt-sleeves. He passed the mess around, forcing the most noble and delicate ladies among his guests to eat it out of his hand. He would even wipe his hands on their frilly dresses, generally taking elaborately lewd aim.

The more squeamish of his guests suffered these thrusts silently; some clapped and cheered at them; and others, surprisingly, thrilled to them. Such is the paradox of the civilized.

Those who suffered from such gross displays attended these affairs as a matter of necessity. Even if one were the highest minister of the realm, it could be—and often was—fatal to snub Rasputin when he called on one to come to dine. It took nothing for Rasputin; one word, however repellent to Nicholas, accomplished his notions.

But these feasts did not occur solely for the satisfaction of Rasputin's baser sensibilities. His dining hall also served as a forum or arena where both the rich and the poverty-stricken could make petitions for special favors. A ribbon-bedecked general, once thrashed by the Grand Duke Nicholas Nicholaievitch on a caprice and demoted several ranks, presented his story to Rasputin and won back his career in one obsequious evening. A high official, banished to wilds of eastern Siberia for embezzling state funds, curried pardon at the expense of his vanity. One man in the ministry might argue for his promotion; another might come to denounce a third, and so on. Complaints were aired, petitions rendered. Jews came forth seeking protection from the anti-Semitic military and from the police. And, of course, the ever-present Russian peasants came, begging for alms and jobs.

Rasputin applied his own procedure to these hearings. He looked upon them not as a chance to amass a fortune, but as a splendid, powerful game. He engineered a petty reorganization of wealth at each dinner, combining his pet project of insulting the high with his compassion for the low. "You generals and officers have been accustomed to privilege!" he would shout. "You have hitherto been first; tonight I shall put you last. Go over to the walls and let my friends, the Jews, dine with me."

And then the high and mighty would be required to attend upon the supper of the poor. When the feast had been consummated, Rasputin would gleefully strip the rich of all their petty cash and unburden the peasants of their notes and bills. Then he would exchange the money and bills, giving the peasants each about a hundred rubles and the rich each a bill or two. Then he would say, "I shall hear all of the Jews and peasants before the generals and the ladies, for I salute the poor; they are better than the rich pigs." And he would send all the poor over to Simanovitsch in the corner, who was charged with dispensing Rasputin's justice. Only after the last pauper gained his mercy did Rasputin begin to hear the petitions of the rich. Many of the petitioners were women, the wives of men mired at some particular level of the ministry but too vain or stupid to seek out favor to aid their advancement. Of these Rasputin demanded only one type of payment—her company in his bed.

This indifference to opinion and morality swelled the ranks of his enemies, but he didn't mind. Whenever he grabbed for power, wine, or flesh, it was always there, and his life became a round of indulgence, orgy, and success.

Withal, Rasputin's ego never swelled beyond its natural proportions. He never played the righteous monk or yielded to the temptation to judge his fellow Russians—other than to insult them, that is. He never asked anyone, rich or poor, "Are you worthy to receive my favor?" In a sweeping act of blind compassion, he assumed the worth of everyone's claim and did his best to satisfy it. He aided even those few wives who clung tenaciously to the ideal of fidelity and refused his demands. And he did it whether they refused him out of real religious impulse or out of a patently obvious disgust of his presence.

Even this altruism, however, arose from a kind of spiritual pride. "Why should I trade a woman for a bag of gold?" he would say. "Am I not powerful enough to gain what I want without money?"

And he was right: he was powerful enough to get both his necessities and his luxuries without the cold touch of the coin. So he shunned the whole business of moneymaking and refused to entangle himself in its commerce.

This is not to say that Rasputin lived on a shoestring. Indeed, his style of life consumed thousands of rubles. Although he remained aloof and unconcerned about the sources of his large income, his style of life certainly made that income a necessity. As Rasputin's trustee, Aaron Simanovitsch had his hands full. The Tsar helped of course. At first this source was light and sporadic, but Simanovitsch finally negotiated an allowance for Rasputin in the order of five thousand rubles per month. Because it had to come from the Treasury and because the Treasury was constantly stretched to fund the labyrinthine bureaucracy which administered the rule of the Tsar over all of Russia, the Tsar could afford no more.

Five thousand made a mere drop in the bucket against the expenses Rasputin ran up in a month. Besides the food bills for his nightly feasts and entertainment bills from the opera and music halls, there was the gargantuan cost of the veritable rivers of wine imbibed at the banquets. Rasputin cared not a whit for these trifles; he had complete faith and trust in Simanovitsch's ability.

Rasputin's profligacy forced Simanovitsch to dip into his own pocket to pay off some of these bills, especially toward the end of the month when Rasputin's reserves were exhausted. Simanovitsch did not mind this in the least, as he cherished his position more than his wealth; and indeed, in the long run, it is difficult to determine whether he lost or gained by such investments. In any case, the influence he wielded enabled him to perform many benevolent actions on behalf of his people, and increasingly this afforded his life the meaning and personal satisfaction any man needs to remain stable and self-respecting.

When a particularly fierce squall whipped up his financial sea, Simanovitsch had no qualms about asking his friends for help. There were a surprising number of Jewish millionaires in Russia in the first two decades of the twentieth century. Men such as Moses Ginsberg, ———— Veychik, ———— Manus, and ———— Kaminka had quietly and prudently steered their course through the many shoals of

Russian commerce during the booming 1890s, and had emerged to form a silent Jewish elite. To be fair, it must be appreciated that their exalted position depended very directly on their unobtrusiveness. Anti-Semitism had been the ruin of the many more prominent, less cautious Russian Jews. The lesson learned, these careful men enjoyed their wealth in private and eagerly took advantage of the rather indirect yet very effective opportunities for philanthropy which Simanovitsch offered them. Thus, with their aid, he was able to ease the burden on his personal resources.

One of Simanovitsch's most ingenious coups was to establish a tradition: when arriving by invitation at one of Rasputin's feasts, guests were accustomed to bring gifts for their host. Simanovitsch asked everyone to refrain from exercising their imagination as to what gifts to bring. Situations like this could very easily deteriorate into an extravagant and wasteful competition to determine who could offer the gaudiest and most ostentatious gift. What use could Rasputin—or Simanovitsch—ever make of a Turkish camel or a cage of Ethiopian lemurs?

Simanovitsch offered the saner and much more practical solution—food. This not only suited his needs, but also offered itself as a test of originality and generosity for those who wished to compete. The poor could also well afford to enter the fray by bearing staples—potatoes, cabbage, carrots, and fresh bread. The richer among his guests could supply Rasputin with the famed Siberian salmon, rich, black caviar, juicy red apples from the orchards of the Crimea, and the manifold varieties of crisp southern wines which Rasputin loved. The only taboos rested on meats, cakes, and—surprisingly—vodka, three items distasteful to the monk's palate.

Simanovitsch's responsibility didn't remain merely financial. During the course of his relationship with Rasputin his concern for the monk widened to include all the emotions of friendship, and led him to assume the unofficial post of watchman. Simanovitsch silently, certainly, and regularly surveyed the entire field of Rasputin's enemies and drew conclusions, which he passed on to his charge when he felt that Rasputin should be aware of them. The greatest tact and delicacy had to be employed in maneuvers such as these, for Rasputin was by no means an avid devotee of strategy. He unequivocally preferred indulging his senses to indulging in intrigue, so that Simanovitsch repeatedly lost these engagements. But he never ceased initiating them when he felt them called for.

One brittley cold evening in December, Simanovitsch joined his friend at a party at Vyrubova's small house near the palace, with precisely the purpose of exhorting him once again to take action against the perpetrators of a tide of rumors which were inundating Court society. Finally Simanovitsch was able to hustle Rasputin into the dumpy little library which occupied the west end of the cottage. Secluded as the library was, the very next morning the particulars of this conversation began their sojourn on the river, borne by no less than five separate mouths, including that of the hostess herself.

Simanovitsch had watched the flow of rumors with much the same studied interest as present-day politicians watch polls. But this autumn they had grown dangerously vicious—or at least Simanovitsch thought they had. The ones impugning the fidelity of the Empress and naming Rasputin her lover could easily be tolerated; they were bound to arise, given Rasputin's intimacy with the Imperial Family. But the one which nettled Simanovitsch into activity challenged the chastity of the Grand Duchess Tatiana and named Rasputin as the culprit. This one could prove dangerous to Nicholas if it floated about too long; the schism in his Court and family was severe enough already. Simanovitsch sensed the drift of the situation as he learned that even the uncles and aunts of Nicholas and Alexandra were passing their own versions of the rumor. He decided he must speak.

"Rasputin, do you know what they are saying about you?"

"Yes—I know their lies," the monk answered brusquely, impatient to end the conversation.

"But it gets worse. Even Nicholas speaks against you. You must act now. Tonight!"

"What can I do? Must I atone for sins I did not commit? It is absurd. I will not."

"I know that you are innocent," Simanovitsch explained sympathetically, "but do the people know? It is those other women—every night a different one at your house. It is they who make you liable. Give them up; give them all up. You cannot continue so—they will not let you."

"They will not let me?" Rasputin shot back. "Why, these women come to me, don't they? I don't go to them. I seek out no one. That talk about Alexandra is all nonsense. And they know it. No one soils the place where he eats; they know that. As for the other talk, the child, it is too much. They are just pigs, swine. I don't even think they really believe it."

"But, Novitch, can't you see how it goes for you? Why, it is not just Russians—all Europe talks of the Tsarina's darling. How can you do this to her? They mock her. Do you wish this? Why don't you stop? Why not cool off now?"

"My friend, as I said, they come to me—I do not go to them. How am I to stop them? Am I to say to Mrs. Suzatka, 'No, Anna, I cannot; they will talk about us.' No, it is absurd. I cannot—I will not reject them. I am a healthy man yet, Simanovitsch. I shall not stop. We shall talk of it no more. They are swine. I shall not freeze for them. First I shall make peace with [Kaiser] Wilhelm, Simanovitsch, and then I shall go to Jerusalem. They will stop talking: I shall make the pilgrimage."

So for all his trouble Simanovitsch received only Rasputin's promise that he would make a holy and public pilgrimage to Jerusalem when the cords of peace united the Kaiser to the Tsar. Of course, he never would. And why should anyone have expected him to have done it? Rasputin enjoyed life in the capital. Nor was he ever guilty of the secret sins ascribed to him; for he lived honestly and sinned openly.

In fact, his relation to the Imperial Family, his life's blood, remained on the surest footing. That he never once did enter the palace when Nicholas was absent is just one of the many manifestations of his respect and devotion to the family. His concern over the talked about marriage of the Grand Duchess Olga to the Grand Duke Dimitri Pavlovitch is yet another. He believed Dimitri's handshake capable of transmitting a severe disease and he spoke to Alexandra about this, warning her not only to discourage the match but to avoid shaking hands with him. Since Rasputin knew that Dimitri was part of the family and that this precaution could not always be observed, he left the Empress with a bunch of Siberian herbs to cleanse her hands and destroy the morbid influences which she would contract.

She believed Rasputin and discouraged Dimitri. And why

shouldn't she believe him? The best doctors of the realm had failed to cure her hemophiliac son, but countless times Rasputin brought his mysterious self into the bedchamber of the suffering Tsarevitch and wrapped him in healing rays. The doctors' science was powerless to stop the blood and quell the pain, but Rasputin's presence and prayers did it. It was that simple—Rasputin could do what others could not.

He became the friend of each member of the family separately. Each found in him a confidence and encouragement which led them to want to confide in him. Since their special position precluded the possibility of the friendships which ordinary men, women, and children form, they cherished his friendship all the more. Alexis especially, isolated by his cruel disease from the healthy child's fields and playgrounds, needed the presence of Rasputin to keep a window of hope open in his little life. Without this, the strain and despair would have crushed him.

Rasputin responded to each member of the family out of the breadth of his personality. With Nicholas he discussed the business and burdens of rulership, thus forming the entente which was the immediate source of his great power. With Alexandra he discussed the boy, giving her constant hope in the possibility of his future. With the children he acted as guide, storyteller, and counsel, standing up for them when they tried to get something out of their tight-fisted mother such as a new dress for Easter or a pretty spring bonnet.

The key to Rasputin's character—whether it was his prodigality at banquets, his success in bed, or his relations to the Tsar and his family—was simply breadth and versatility. He was a man reared in the expanse of the Siberian wilderness, whose personality took the variegated and limitless aspects of wild land.

SIX

In Tsarist Russia, as in other countries of the West, the Jewish community lived uniquely apart from the other members of the corporate state. This ancient distinction of separateness, of meanness, of alienation showed itself in the fabric of organized society. These unfortunates were made to live in close-packed clusters in the poverty-stricken and sordid ghettoes which formed the bowels of each city, town, and village, down to the least hamlet of the empire. To live in the filth and starvation of rickety tenements and muddy, rutted streets meant only a life struggle in which to desire was to despair.

Yet there were some, as there always would be, who dared to desire, who braved the ancient onus of defeat and abjection, and who set out to manage their way out of this demeaning milieu. Their way was strewn with an appalling array of obstacles and discouragements. Their eager souls had to be wrapped toughly and thickly, or else they would capitulate before the hatred and abuse which awaited them in the outside world.

But the physical and emotional onslaught was the least part of the battle. A whole host of Imperial pronouncements, administrative decrees, and common-law traditions wove an entangling mesh about any Jew's attempted escape into decency and snared his least effort before it began. From cradle to grave, restrictions kept the Jew in his bondage. The youth was debarred access to the university; the young man exempted from trading licenses; and the whole family herded into special residential settlements.

Aaron Simanovitsch, by dint of fortune, skill, and sense, had risen above this too common fate. But he had never once forgotten his humble origins and never excluded from his sensibilities his relationship to his people. His struggles for their cause were to be long and torturous too, for he was but a single character faced with a multitude of antagonists.

In truth, all the Gentiles of the realm were his enemies, from the high to the low, for the persecution of the Jews could not have gone on as it did without the bigoted passions of the great mass of men to provide it with its energy. Without them, a pogrom could not rage. But one cannot hold an entire people responsible, either in fiction or in fact, and so we must consider their leaders as the palpable sparks which initiated the flame.

The most ignoble actor in the anti-Semitic troupe was a cousin of Nicholas II, the Grand Duke Nicholas Nicholaievitch. Like his Imperial first cousin Alexander III, Nicholas was blessed with a Herculean stature and towered over the shoulders of ordinary men. But his soul burned unnaturally and malevolently; he was almost bestial in his fury and savagery. As a youth he thirsted for the sight of blood, and as a young officer he made a great name for himself as a warrior against the Turks. In 1878, when the Turkish wars were done and peace had settled on the country, he bridled against the stately life of leisure and his blood lust carried him deep into the jungles of Asian Russia where he hunted the wild game which slunk through the thick vegetation. The great World War spread a vast and thrilling opportunity before him and he entered it fiercely and darkly. His victims were numberless: Jews, Galicians, Poles, and Germans. Any charge would do: espionage, desertion, collaboration—the war provided many easy excuses for execution. Men, women, and children were shot en masse at his order or hanged individually if his troops' ammunition was depleted.

Even his own subordinates didn't escape his sadistic wrath. Aroused, he could beat them bloody with his bare fists, and his fury extended even to generals whom he had only recently decorated for their valor or loyalty. His tantrums caused many embarrassments and much misery. But they were tolerated with a tacit acknowledgment of his genius as a military strategist. He was a tainted anachronism, an Attila come alive in Russian flesh, a dangerous man; but just then Russia needed him to direct his passionate insanity against the Kaiser's invading forces.

His Chief of the General Staff, General Yanushkevitch, shared his hatred of the Jews, although less intensely. A cousin of his had had dealings with Simanovitsch and some other prominent members of the small Jewish elite. The cousin's estate in Tula had been set as collateral against a 400,000 ruble debt; friends of Simanovitsch's owned the territorial bank which had made the loan. Yanushkevitch's cousin could not pay them and Simanovitsch's friends would not dissolve the debt. So his cousin lost the estate and Yanushkevitch nourished the affront to his family.

General Yanushkevitch's cohort, General Ruzsky, was variously the commander of the Northwest and the Pleskau Fronts. His conviction that all Jews were spies overrode the dictates of his conscience and allowed him to send his officers out on missions of vengeance. These forays into the land about Galicia registered in the log book as "investigative patrols." One of his junior officers once remained out in the fields for three days, giving no information concerning his whereabouts or progress. He was taken for dead, but later returned at the head of his squadron of Cossacks with the blood caked on the length of their swords. He explained to an approving Ruzsky that it had taken longer than anticipated to exterminate the espionage agents in the surrounding villages; the Jewish population had been more numerous than they had thought.

Against these martial devils the Jewish population had little defense. Yet they did have protectors, if they could only reach them. It would cost them all they had, but if they could make the journey across the Russian steppes to St. Petersburg, for instance, they would find comfort and solace in the household of Aaron Simanovitsch.

Simanovitsch had constructed what was nothing less than a corporate agency of mercy. His organization spread its influence all over Russia, gathering both commercial and social data, centralizing a welter of complaint and protest, and focusing pressure on the pliant pieces in both the governmental and financial machinery. His agents kept him in constant communication with the local Jewish centers and provided him with immediate warning of impending tragedies.

If he received from a correspondent a telegram reading:

WE ARE WORRIED ABOUT YOUR HEALTH. TELEGRAPH US,

he immediately contacted the local authorities and reminded them of this business contingency or that pending promotion or of his personal ability to decide upon the course of their private economies and their governmental careers. He would instruct these subservient officials to invite to dinner the representatives and rabbis of the local Jewish settlement, thus calming down their fears and brushing away their anxieties. Of course, he also commanded them to take whatever actions would lead to the speedy dissolution of the tensions which were building toward a pogrom. His correspondent then got a telegram:

MORNING HOPE TO BE HEALTHY. IMMEDIATELY GIVE NEWS WHEN I CAN LEAVE HOUSE,

whereupon they knew he had acted and that help was near. Giers of Minsk and Lubimov of Vilna were just two of the many governors who deflected incipient pogroms upon Simanovitsch's orders.

In the beginning Rasputin would not listen to a word of the Jewish lament. He was infused daily with the ripe anti-Semitic opinions of Nicholas and his ministers. This flood of personal propaganda led him, too, to believe that Jewish youths were nothing but revolutionaries and that Jewish liberation was a certain threat to the Empire.

But his friend Simanovitsch constantly expatiated upon the plight of his coreligionists, and tale after tale, day after day, he expounded their situation and explained their predicament. He inundated Rasputin with facts and figures that exploded the fictions of Nicholas and his close-minded ministers. And finally, against the onslaught of Simanovitsch's persuasion, Rasputin's animosity ebbed and his better instincts emerged in a tentative bond of affection and sympathy for Simanovitsch's people. Of course, the bond was tender and new, and Rasputin's actions in behalf of the Jews were at first mere gestures of support.

Simanovitsch's own efforts in the great capital were directed into three areas—business, education, and travel. In order to obtain licenses to participate in the various urban trades, a Jew had to pass an examination sponsored by the St. Petersburg Chamber of Commerce. Simanovitsch kept in constant communication with the members of this body. Through financial and outright pecuniary levers, he managed to place men on the board who were responsive to his desires. In this way he was able to launch many of his people into the prosperity of urban commerce. He set up an organization to process the many requests for travel permits which came to him from men who needed to make business trips or wanted to emigrate to St. Petersburg or Moscow to set themselves up as tradesmen. He honored all these requests equally and processed them quickly through his unofficial bureau, which then made the necessary accommodations with local authorities.

In their quest for admission to higher institutions of learning, the number of youths who applied for his aid grew yearly, but here the problems were most exasperating. For how was one to bear down upon a professor who scorned even the mention of commercial involvements? These academic men were securely distant from Simanovitsch's world of business and impervious to the baser persuasions. But in this area Rasputin was able to provide the coercion, for although the professors were secure from the vicissitudes of finance, their positions depended upon the grace of the Court. Intractable ministers of education were likely to receive a note such as this:

> My dear kind minister, Mama wishes that these Jewish students may study in their homeland so that they do not need to go to foreign countries where they are made into revolutionaries.
>
> Yours in the Savior,
> Father Grigori

"Mama," of course, meant the Tsarina. These letters from Rasputin were sent not only to the ministers but to others who had influence at the university or school. Many professors, court ladies, and clergy aided Simanovitsch's purposes when this type of pressure arrived in their morning mail.

During the Great War, Simanovitsch's special concern became the draft. He knew the fate that waited for the young Jewish draftee in the regiments of Nicholas and Ruzsky, and if he could help a boy avoid it he spared no effort. His principal goal, admission of the boy to a high school or religious institution, not only procured a deferment but also provided the boy with the basis of a future career. Simanovitsch even created a new institution, The Rural Economic and Hydro-Technological Institute, to handle the surplus of eligible students. Of its enrollment of six hundred boys, seventy percent were Jews, enrolled because of Simanovitsch's influence with his friend the Rector Balitsky. Balitsky had been Chancery Chief to the Secretary of State Kryzhanovsky, who in turn had wanted to be introduced to Rasputin. Simanovitsch's condition for arranging the meeting had been Balitsky's appointment as rector.

If his move to enroll a boy was thwarted—as some were bound to be under the pressure of such vast numbers of applicants— Simanovitsch made an appeal to the draft commission headquartered in the city of Luga. Since Rasputin had arranged the appointment of many of these commissioners, they could be influenced by an appeal. The special coded signs which Simanovitsch had placed on the papers of these recruits marked them as his favorites and ensured their rejection by the board.

While Aaron Simanovitsch didn't deprecate the worth of these efforts, he knew that they remained mere piecemeal achievements. He often brooded over the lot of the Jews in Russia and considered it his personal responsibility to bring a general and all-encompassing elevation of Jewish rights to his people. In his ameliorative plans he counted heavily on the help of one of his confederates, the millionaire Moses Ginsberg.

Ginsberg had made his fortune in the trading industry of Port Arthur, in eastern Siberia. When he learned of the persecutions and atrocities of Grand Duke Nicholas Nicholaievitch, he became ill with remorse and grief. After he conversed with Simanovitsch, the two men decided that the time had come for a concerted Jewish effort to defend and protect against the encroachment of their human rights.

They decided to organize a pool of Jewish money which could be used to finance a continual lobby seeking reform from the ministries in St. Petersburg. They would convoke, they said, a congress of Jewish representatives and involve them in a concerted effort. Their greatest hope lay in their ability to convince Rasputin to come out freely for their cause. To this end a meeting was set up with a number of prominent Jews and Rasputin. The occasion was worked around a dinner party at Ginsberg's home.

As Rasputin entered the living room, Ginsberg's guests cheered him with a rousing tide of applause and shouts. Their fervor impressed the peasant, and their tales of woe decided him in their cause. He told them they must support the efforts of his good friend Simanovitsch, and not shrink so coyly from the payment of bribes—for this was the method of their day, as it had been of their fathers', and of their grandfathers' before them. The meeting was a complete success, and the only man who suffered was Ginsberg himself. His young, attractive wife caught Rasputin's piercing eye, and during dinner Rasputin carried on a lively conversation with her from the adjacent seat. Ginsberg knew of Rasputin's charm and feared that his naive mate might fall victim to the earthy man's potent spell. But his agitation diminished as Simanovitsch interposed himself between the couple; he, too, knew Rasputin's capabilities and wished to forestall any possible embarrassments.

It was long after this meeting that a situation developed that gave the Jews a chance to test their new resolve. A group of some two hundred Jewish men had taken courses and passed examinations which allowed them to practice dentistry in St. Petersburg. Along with their licenses they received permits to reside in the Jewish settlement of the city. These latter documents had been the objects of their endeavors; they had no desire to be dentists, but had wanted merely the privilege of living in the city. But when this subterfuge was discovered, they were arrested and sentenced to death by hanging.

Simanovitsch convoked his unofficial Jewish congress and they all met with Rasputin to decide on what action to take. When Rasputin affirmed that the Minister of Justice at that time, Shcheglovitov, hated him no less than he hated Jews, the delegates' hopes sank. But Simanovitsch proposed an alternative route to a pardon—through the Tsar himself.

This course offered few encouragements, as all knew, for the Tsar professed a vehement anti-Semitism. Since childhood his intimate associates—nurses, tutors, valets, maids, relatives, friends, and, later, his ministers—had drilled into his head the tenets of this prejudice. Only fools would hope that it might be waived in the superstitious atmosphere of the present Court. Nevertheless, eventually they would have to start penetrating Nicholas' obstinacy, and there was no worthier cause to bring to him than this. And so they resolved to proffer a petition to the Tsar on the next Sunday.

Rasputin accompanied Simanovitsch, the bearer of the petition, to the early Sunday services at Tsarskoye Selo. When the worship ended, all the Imperial party repaired to Vyrubova's for a merry breakfast. During the meal, Vyrubova, who was in on the ulterior purpose of Simanovitsch's presence, leaned over to Nicholas' ear and said, "Your Majesty, Aaron Simanovitsch has honored us with his presence."

Nicholas looked up from his eggs and searched out the familiar face from among the two lines of faces down the length of the banquet table. Spotting him next to Tatiana, he cried, "Simanovitsch! What then have you to say to me?"

"Your Imperial Majesty, forgive me for defiling the purity of this day," said Simanovitsch, hanging fire, "but I have vainly shown your most esteemed wife, the Empress, a most remarkable specimen of diamond. It is no less than one hundred carats, and set handsomely as well. I did not wish to let it go before you had the opportunity of examining such a beautiful stone."

With this little speech Simanovitsch fished the sparkling gem from his pocket to present it to the Tsar. But Nicholas interrupted his gesture. "Simanovitsch, you know we cannot indulge ourselves in such opulent expenses while the war rages. What, then, is the meaning of this?"

Suddenly Rasputin raised his head and purred, "It is the Jews, Nicholas."

Nicholas, having anticipated the reason for Simanovitsch's presence, was prepared for this, and when the jeweler finished telling him in very moving and eloquent words the nature of his errand, the Tsar surprised everyone present by admitting the strength of his arguments.

"I do not wish to send the angel of death into the homes of my war-afflicted people," he said. "Enough tragedy comes of itself. Go! Bring the petition to Taneiev; he will carry out my pardon."

And so Simanovitsch went to the Chief of the Chancellery and the two hundred men were returned to their families.

People everywhere were stunned. No one had ever heard of such a victory. And accomplished by a Jew! Gratitude flowed through the hearts of all the people in the settlement, and they took up a collection to send gifts to Rasputin and Simanovitsch. They managed to gather eight hundred rubles and brought Rasputin a sable fur. To Simanovitsch they sent a honeycomb, a bottle of red wine, and a silver bowl.

For the first time the Jewish people of Russia were infused with a sense of pride and cohesion. There was a rejuvenation of spirits and a revival of the rich cultural expressions which had been dampened by the onset of the war and the persecutions which attended it.

The most illustrious example of this cultural renaissance arose from a conversation between Simanovitsch and the entrepreneur Alexander Fishon. Fishon told Simanovitsch about his interest in organizing an opera company. He was prepared to work out the details and finance the scheme, but the law forbade Jewish theater, even in the settlements, so he needed help from Simanovitsch to get permission.

Simanovitsch offered to do what he could about it and asked for a list of the proposed cast members. When he received the list of about forty names, he brought it with him on his next visit to Tsarskoye Selo. At the dinner table he got Nicholas' attention and asked, "Your Majesty, I have here on this piece of paper the names of forty members of my community who are distinguished by the

possession of certain thespian talents. I was hoping that during the
holidays I could present them in a show in my home. As I realize
your concern that the Jewish theater can give birth to certain
dangerous ideas, I have taken the precaution to ensure the presence
of Bishop Isidor—he is the prelate who presides over our settlement, Your Majesty—and he could guarantee that these offensive
ideas don't show their heads in the production."

"But," Alexandra interrupted, speaking to no one in particular,
"how can a Jewish production be suspicious or offensive?"

Nicholas didn't take up this point and seemed willing to consider
the possibility, so Simanovitsch added, "Yes, and Rasputin has said
he would come, and Minister Stürmer, too."

Alexandra seemed ready to grant the affair her sanction. "What
do you want us to do, Simanovitsch?" she asked.

"We need the Imperial signature on our petition, Your Majesty,"
he replied.

Alexandra didn't even wait for Nicholas' reaction, but took the
paper from Simanovitsch and wrote on it, "Ratified, signed, Alexandra."

The Tsar merely shrugged and continued eating his meal.

Simanovitsch gladly accepted the document and the next day
brought it to the City Supervisor, an obese man named Vlatnikov.
Mr. Vlatnikov was shocked by the paper—the ruling against theater
had been long and stringently enforced throughout its history. But
he knew Simanovitsch and didn't present any difficulty. The next
stop was police headquarters, where Simanovitsch filled out the
necessary forms in triplicate.

Fishon's cast arrived in St. Petersburg the next month, and in their
honor Simanovitsch assembled a number of dignitaries for a reception in his home. Rasputin was there, Stürmer was there, Isidor was
there. Protopopov, the Interior Minister, came along with his
assistant, Balitsky, and General Boris Globachev, the Chief of the
Political Police, came too. The cast were more than a little surprised
to see such an agglomeration of dignity under a Jewish roof, and
everyone enjoyed himself immensely. The actors took special
pleasure in the attention bestowed upon them at last and everyone

enjoyed the rich wines, liquors, and foods which Simanovitsch apportioned so lavishly.

Afterward, all repaired in carriages provided by the host to the German Katherinin Club for the special show. The prima donna, Clara Young, headed the troupe, and her singing crowned the efforts of a generally sterling cast. The applause deafened them and brought tears to their eyes; it was the first they had heard in too many years.

The reception and show were a brilliant success, and later on Fishon heard with incredulity that permission was granted to establish a permanent theater in the district. As the opera house distinguished itself with the favor of the Tsar and Tsarina's attendance, the troupe was also granted permission to tour all of Russia. Nicholas had not been able to withstand the tremendous effects of Miss Young's virtuosity, and like everyone else who came to see her, he succumbed to the magic of her art.

But Simanovitsch did not forget that throughout this period the Great War was raging. He could not, for every day people came to plead with him to help them rescue this or that relative.

Doctor Lipert's case presents a most interesting example of this type of operation. It was the first such case which Simanovitsch and Rasputin worked on. The doctor had been taken prisoner on the western front during the first German offensive. His wife, a relative of Countess Witte, had heard of Simanovitsch and went to him for help. Her husband was an old and sickly man, she told Simanovitsch; he'd die if he wasn't returned soon.

Simanovitsch called Rasputin, who agreed to meet with her the next morning at breakfast. Mrs. Lipert became extremely excited at this prospect and spent a restless night of anticipation. The meeting transpired at the peasant's breakfast table.

"What can we do?" Rasputin asked Simanovitsch. "How can we proceed?"

"Why not bring the case to the Minister of Foreign Affairs, Sazonov?"

Rasputin blushed, and after a moment's hesitation said, "No, Simanovitsch, we cannot go to Minister Sazonov. He has talked to Nicholas about me. He has tried to turn Nicholas against me. He is my enemy! How can I ask a favor of my enemy? No, I can't. We cannot go to the Foreign Minister."

"But, Rasputin," Simanovitsch countered, "there is no way around Sazonov. We cannot negotiate with the Germans without his learning about it. And how could we bargain? Can we offer to trade any of our prisoners? No, we must approach the Minister. You must send Mrs. Lipert to him with a letter."

Rasputin haggled some more with his friend, but in the end he was persuaded to scribble off the following message to be delivered to Minister Sazonov by Mrs. Lipert:

> My dear kind man, Grant help to a man languishing in a German prison. Demand one Russian for one German. God helps us to save ourselves.
>
> Signed,
> Novitch Rasputin

The next day the woman carried the note to the Minister. When he had perused the missive, he looked up through his rimless spectacles and blinked.

"Certainly I can accomplish this exchange for you, Madame," he said. "In fact, I would have done it for you even without this foolish letter. But I have seven names on my list before your husband's name, so we must have patience and trust in God. It will happen as soon as possible. Trust me." He smiled lavishly, a gold inlay gleaming on his front tooth.

"But Minister Sazonov, my husband is old and very ill. He must be sent home now, or he will surely die in those dank rooms," replied Mrs. Lipert.

"Do not worry, Mrs. Lipert. We shall have your husband home as soon as it can be arranged. Tomorrow, in fact, I go to the Red Cross to begin negotiations. I shall do everything in my power to return the doctor to you at the earliest possible moment. Don't fret anymore. He will survive. Now you must excuse me, for I have much work to do."

When Mrs. Lipert left Sazonov's office she reported directly to Rasputin, who became angry at the Minister for his insolence but refrained from displaying his emotions. Eight days later Mrs. Lipert returned to tell him that Sazonov hadn't done anything yet, and this news brought out a week's pent-up wrath.

> Hear me this time, Minister. I have sent a lady to you. God knows what you have said to her. Let what she asks for happen: make this exchange immediately. Only then shall everything be all right with you and me. If you refuse me twice I shall not stand for it. You know my worth to the Loved Ones. You have felt my power already. Do not tempt me. I will strike.
>
> Signed,
> Rasputin

Mrs. Lipert trembled as she entered Sazonov's office for the second time. She felt awfully small and weak, yet her love and fear for her husband helped her gather her wits and emotions together and address the minister. "Mr. Minister, I am Mrs. Lipert," she began. "I have come to see you about my husband, the doctor. Have you done anything about his release?"

"Yes, I know it is you, Mrs. Lipert," replied Sazonov. "And I am working on your husband's release. You must have patience; these negotiations are a delicate matter, and the list of prisoners is very long."

Mrs. Lipert made a quick decision and handed him Rasputin's corrosive letter. His countenance turned crimson as he read it, and when he was finished he looked up at her in pure outrage. Then, before he had the chance to vent his wrath, Mrs. Lipert—in an inspired move—picked up the telephone and rang up Rasputin.

Just as the peasant's voice sounded on the line, the plucky woman thrust the receiver into Sazonov's hands. The Minister, hearing that it was Rasputin at the other end of the line, fumbled and brought out, "My dear Father Grigori, what kind of letter have you sent with this good lady? Are you angry with me?"

Rasputin commanded a sense of the ironic. "Why, whatever gave you that impression, Minister Sazonov? Of course I am not the least bit angry with you. I don't honestly know what gave you that idea.

Perhaps you feel guilty about slighting me? Your reluctance does offend me, you know. But I am not angry, Minister. I know how difficult a minister's job is these days. Nicholas is so very fickle, isn't he, Minister Sazonov? He turns against so many now, doesn't he? But how would you know about these things? You have been on good terms with the Tsar recently, haven't you? I hope, Minister, that you don't omit to do anything which could topple such a promising career. You do intend continuing at your post, do you not, Mr. Sazonov?"

Yes, Mr. Sazonov told Rasputin, he certainly did intend to continue on at his post and he also counted on the good father's support in the coming weeks. These negotiations with the enemy were so very delicate, you see. The conversation was ended after some further sweetly styled phrases of agreement and concord.

Two weeks later Doctor Lipert was enjoying his wife's cooking.

When Simanovitsch set out to help his people, there was often a great deal at stake. In one case involving the Poles, for instance, hundreds of lives hung in the balance. General Gruselo, conforming to the general pattern of military depravity, had charged a number of the Polish population with collaboration with the enemy. He claimed they had transmitted information about troop movements to Germany over the telegraph lines, and his solution was to exile each head of each Polish household to Siberia. By the time Father Kasimir, deacon of the Polish community in St. Petersburg, could ask Simanovitsch for advice, the men had already begun the hard journey east.

Simanovitsch set up a meeting with Rasputin, which the priest attended dressed in the official garb of his order. This little show of respect impressed Rasputin, as did Father Kasimir's earnest and obsequious manner and, of course, his tragic tale.

"The charges are absurd, absolutely absurd," shouted the peasant. "Indeed, I will help. We are all Slavs. We must help each other. Bring the women and children into St. Petersburg," he ordered. "Simanovitsch shall find homes for them."

Simanovitsch agreed that this was entirely feasible. The sad group of women and children were brought in and from their melancholy

A. Simanovitsch

The Winter Palace in St. Petersburg, capital of Imperial Russia. Although this was the Tsar's official residence, he lived mainly at the Alexander Palace, Tsarskoye Selo.

Tsarskoye Selo, fifteen miles south of St. Petersburg

The Emperor Nicholas II and the Empress Alexandra, with their five children. From left to right: the Grand Duchesses Olga and Marie, the Emperor, the Empress, the Grand Duchess Anastasia, the Tsarevitch Alexis, and the Grand Duchess Tatiana.

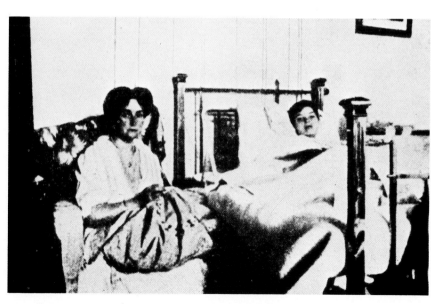

The Empress Alexandra and the Tsarevitch Alexis during one of his recuperations from hemophiliac bleeding.

A typical peasant dwelling

The House of Grigori Rasputin in Pokrovskoye, Siberia

Grigori Rasputin

Anna Vyrubova, confidante of the Empress and friend of Rasputin, who introduced him to Simanovitsch.

Grigori Rasputin (seated fourth from left), surrounded by ladies of the Imperial Court. Anna Vyrubova is standing fifth from left.

One of the daily gatherings at Rasputin's St. Petersburg apartment. Rasputin is seated second from left.

The interior of a prison

A peasant in chains

A prisoner being whipped

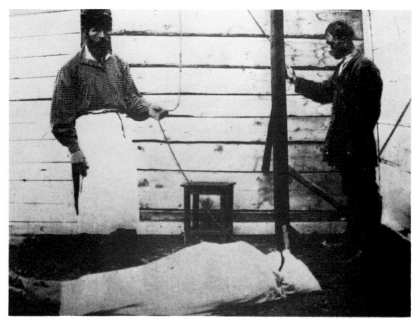

A corpse shrouded after being hanged

ranks Rasputin chose five women and five children as representatives.

Although Nicholas was at the front at this time, the small, doleful party made the fifteen-mile walk to the Tsar's residence at Tsarskoye Selo to meet Alexandra, who received them in her military hospital and was moved to tears at their story.

"What can I do, Father?" she asked Rasputin.

"Send their petition to Nicholas," he said.

"Better yet, I shall take it to him myself," the Empress volunteered. "I am leaving to go to headquarters tomorrow. Bring me the petition in the morning."

Simanovitsch spent the remainder of the day searching for attorneys to write up the petition. There were plenty around, but no one wanted the job: it was neither proper nor prudent to affix one's name to a petition on behalf of foreign peoples. So finally, at midnight, with a score of refusals ringing in his ears, Simanovitsch called on his eldest son, who was a student of law, and together they labored into the night, preparing the document.

Alexandra presented the petition to Nicholas, and he accepted it. The exiles were returned within three weeks.

Although there were many times when Simanovitsch tried to engineer such reunions as these, not all of his work was fruitful. His defeats came from every quarter but by far they came most consistently from the front, where Grand Duke Nicholas Nicholaievitch presided over a systematic decimation of Jewish and foreign peoples. One of the most heinous of his crimes was perpetrated against the *zadikim* (or rabbis) of southern Ukraina. Soon after the army occupied this area they experienced a defeat. The Jews were about their business of celebrating Passover, but Nicholas Nicholaievitch declared that they were responsible for the defeat. They had given away his troop movements, he accused, by flashing encoded information on the blades of their windmills and thus were all guilty of espionage.

Cossacks raced into the villages which dotted the wheat-filled plains and arrested each local *zadik* and brought him to the central town. The men were given five minutes' warning, were not allowed to pack any warm clothing, and were not even allowed to say good-bye to their families. When they were all rounded up, the soldiers packed them into cattle-cars and sent them on their way to Siberia. None of the townsfolk were permitted to follow the train and mark its progress; nobody was told its destination.

The people were frantic. They sent Halperin, cantor of the synagogue in Lemberg, to St. Petersburg to enlist the aid of Aaron Simanovitsch. When he heard the case he went immediately to the St. Petersburg authorities, but they demanded documented proof of the tragedy. Everyone had to wait for three weeks while these papers traveled to the capital, but when they did arrive, Nicholas immediately granted pardon.

The telegram was sent to all the stations in Siberia where the train was thought to pass. But the train had never shown up in Siberia. When it reached the feet of the Urals, Grand Duke Nicholas had ordered that it be shunted onto a side track. The *zadikim* were left in the freezing, fetid cars to die of frostbite and starvation.

Tragedies such as this entered frequently into the homes of the Jews during the war. The Grand Duke's homicidal efforts sent chills down their spines when they thought of the millions who died at his urging. Many Jews felt that Nicholas Nicholaievitch was on the verge of exterminating them from the face of Russia. Even the influence of Aaron Simanovitsch did not dissolve their fears; it gave them hope, of course, but a crippling fatalism corroded away their retaliatory spirit.

Nevertheless, the leaders of the Jews were determined to fight, even if their people were disillusioned. They had seen that advances could be pushed through a hostile bureaucracy. Hadn't they resurrected the Jewish theater, increased the population in the universities and in the trades, and won a number of contests with the Tsar's ministers? They took pride in this work, especially in the work of Aaron Simanovitsch. They didn't believe that this was the "pride that goeth before a fall," but rather, that it was the beginning of a modern Jewish uplifting, a new era of liberation.

SEVEN

During the early years of the war, Tsar Nicholas II ruled from his Imperial palace at Tsarskoye Selo. But he always itched to remove to the front, where his cousin the Grand Duke reigned. He wanted to command the Imperial forces himself and to lead his people to glorious victory.

Simanovitsch was aware of the Tsar's yearning; indeed, anyone close to the Imperial couple could see the restlessness which characterized their lives during these years. Simanovitsch decided to take advantage of the Tsar's longing to head his troops, for he had decided that the time had come to do something about the Grand Duke. Simanovitsch resolved to bring about Nicholas Nicholaievitch's fall, even if it cost him his own life. The Grand Duke was a scourge to the Jews, and Simanovitsch thought destiny demanded that he play the avenging angel.

But how? How could he bring down a man when even the Tsar quavered at the thought of contending with him? Simanovitsch may have thought back to those early days in Berlin when he was a young, rich exile. One day in the early part of the fragrant German spring, when the effulgence of the new life about him made a sweet balm for his nerves, he had bumped into an old acquaintance from his university days while walking in the beer gardens. The two had whiled away the afternoon sipping the mellow bock beer, discoursing upon their recent histories, and expatiating upon the present stock of their theories, ideas, and dreams.

The young man was a doctor of medicine, a psychiatrist, and the conversation inevitably touched upon the young man's field of endeavor. Simanovitsch introduced the subject when he asked his friend about his theories concerning volition: "And Herr Doctor, what does your fine science say about my will? Is there any such tissue in my frame? Or is the question of free will another casualty of the advance of science? Come, you must enlighten me."

"My friend," said the young doctor, "the mind of man is a mysterious object still; I am afraid it will always elude the tentacles of the curious. For how can a cup contain more than its volume?— and how can man's mind transcend its limits and review its own self? As for the will, of course, we do have a will. Don't I speak to you now of my own choice? Must we not all continually decide from among a pool of possibility? There are limits, of course. My early decisions effect my later decisions; and both are effected by the decisions of others; and in turn the decisions of others are effected by my decisions. But the greatest influence on our decision-making is not the past and its store of choices-made; it is the immediate, throbbing present with its store of precious desire. It is amazing: most of our strongest desires elude our consciousness. And there-fore, the strongest influences on our decision-making are unknown to us. So to this extent our wills are in bondage; but the master of our wills is our own desires. When we know our desires, then we become free."

Excited by his friend's words, Simanovitsch replied, "Then if someone else were privy to our unconscious desires, he could exert a strangely powerful influence on us?"

"Well," said his friend, "I suppose in general he could—but let's not forget the complexity of desire, and of decisions. Man's behavior is nothing if not richly complex and difficult to pin down to single causes and simple motivations. But I suppose that if you knew my secret desires you could influence me in that direc-tion. Why, does that shock you, Simanovitsch? Isn't this idea embod-ied in the character known to us as the Christian devil? Doesn't Satan's knowledge of our secret desires give him his hellish power over us?" And both Jews had a good laugh in the name of this Gentile nemesis.

Simanovitsch may have recalled this conversation now, on the eve of his battle, Tsar Nicholas over Grand Duke Nicholas Nicho-laievitch, mulling over in his mind the personalities of the three people he had to deal with—primarily—Nicholas, Alexandra, and Rasputin. How could he best influence them to be aligned against the Grand Duke? The situation was difficult indeed.

Nicholas Nicholaievitch's own wife, Anastasia, had been the one who discovered Rasputin when he was chopping wood at the monastery. The Grand Duke himself had favored the monk with his hospitality and, until his departure for the front, had always received Rasputin gladly. This friendly connection had to be severed, of course, if Simanovitsch was to succeed, and the only way he could see to break the link between the Grand Duke and Rasputin lay in provoking the Grand Duke beyond his limit. Since Nicholas Nicho-laievitch had a low threshold of endurance, this task reduced itself to presenting him with one too many petitions—which could easily be arranged.

During the fighting, thousands of German Imperial citizens were captured and sent to Siberia to work in the mines. Simanovitsch persuaded Rasputin to ask the Grand Duke to cancel the banishment of a few of these men.

At first the Grand Duke did this as a matter of course. But then he started to receive petitions to grant these exiles Russian citizenship. Simanovitsch kept petitions flying at the Grand Duke in a continual escalation of supplication. Finally when Jewish names started to appear on them, the Grand Duke decided he had had enough.

Simanovitsch received the following telegram:

APPROVED. FOR THE LAST TIME. RECEPTION OF ANOTHER PETITION WILL CAUSE YOUR REPEAT YOUR EXILE TO SIBERIA.

NICHOLAS

Simanovitsch jumped for joy. He telephoned Rasputin and told him he was coming over with urgent business. When he arrived it was just four o'clock in the summer afternoon and the early setting sun lent a purple glow to the Russian sky.

"We are in ruin," he cried. "Serious trouble! The Grand Duke has refused to grant us any more petitions. He has even threatened to exile *me* to Siberia! Here, read this telegram." And he showed Rasputin the slip of paper. "Well, what do you think?" he said, when his friend had read it.

"Simanovitsch, Simanovitsch," chuckled the peasant, "you are too easily excited. Here, drink this glass of wine. It will calm your nerves. There is nothing to worry about. It is all merely a slight misunderstanding. I'll go to headquarters and straighten it out with Nicholas Nicholaievitch. Here, post this telegram for me."

Rasputin sent Simanovitsch out to send his telegram to the Grand Duke informing him of Rasputin's intention to pay a visit. He waited for the return and when he had it, he had to walk the long way back to Rasputin's house to give himself time to conceal his utter glee. It said:

COME. AND I'LL HANG YOU.

NICHOLAS

When Rasputin read the telegram, his eyes at once clouded over and his face became crimson. "Simanovitsch," he said, "you are right. Nicholas is a dangerous man. We must bring him down."

"My friend," replied Simanovitsch, "I am worried for us both. The Grand Duke is a powerful man. We must move with caution."

"Men like me, my friend, are born but once in a hundred years. I cannot do everything. But I can do what I need to do. Do not fear. The Grand Duke will fall."

"How do you propose to get him?" inquired Simanovitsch.

"We must convince the Tsar to assume command of the front and to send the Grand Duke south to the Caucasus, where he will be able to do no harm."

"Exactly as I thought!" shouted the elated Jew. "But how does His Majesty stand on this question?"

"He wants to lead his troops," said the peasant. "But his ministers rant and rave against him every time he brings it up. They've all threatened to resign if he does it. His mother speaks against the proposition too. She tells him that it would be catastrophic to leave the government in Alexandra's hands. They are all afraid that I will then control the government. Nicholas is afraid of them. So he waits."

"But, Rasputin," said Simanovitsch, "suppose each day Alexandra were to urge him to stand up to them and be off where he belongs—at the head of his people. Wouldn't this help him make up his mind?"

"Of course it would," Rasputin returned. "But Mama doesn't know herself what she wants. After all, perhaps she is afraid to be left here alone, with Papa so far away."

"But Novitch," Simanovitsch went on, pursuing his quarry, "couldn't you show her that she has most to fear from the Grand Duke himself? Doesn't she know that Nicholas Nicholaievitch wants one day to be crowned as Nicholas III? Can't you work on her fears of this man?"

"Yes, Simanovitsch, the Tsarina knows these dangers," Rasputin answered. "She has spoken to me before about Nicholas Nicholaievitch. She once asked me if I knew anything about those rumors which said that it was he who had hired those two gardeners to hurt Alexis. Yes, she can be persuaded to speak to Nicholas against him. This is a good idea. But perhaps we should not rest at that. Perhaps more has to be done. We shall see."

One day the next week Simanovitsch called on Rasputin for another of their familiar morning tête-à-têtes. When he entered the dining hall he found Rasputin crouched in front of the great fireplace with three empty bottles of wine already at his feet. The peasant kept staring into the flames, not even noticing Simanovitsch's presence. All of a sudden he jumped up and shouted, "I shall triumph!" and went into some kind of pantomime. His body contorted as if he were wrestling with a beast.

Simanovitsch had never seen him in such a state, and he stayed to watch over him. Through the day Rasputin continued to down bottle after bottle of warm port, abstaining from any solid nourishment. Intermittently, he would go into his phantom struggles and cry out in a weird voice, "I shall conquer him—I shall triumph over him!" Toward evening, he went out to the baths to cleanse himself and retired without eating dinner and without seeing any of his visitors.

Simanovitsch helped him to his bedroom. Before they entered that room, Rasputin dashed into his workroom and scribbled a few words onto a piece of paper. Simanovitsch saw him put the scrap under his pillow when he got into bed. Thinking that the note was just some sort of reminder, Simanovitsch left the room and spent the night on a cot in the kitchen.

Early the next morning, he was awakened by the lively movements of his friend as he prepared their breakfast.

"Good morning, Simanovitsch," he cried, "did you sleep well last night? Here, the coffee will be done in a minute or two."

Simanovitsch was amazed. His friend was the only man he knew who could drink twenty quarts of wine one day and wake up refreshed and affectionate the next. It seemed against nature.

During breakfast, Rasputin took out the note he had made the previous night, ripped it up into small pieces, and tossed them into the hearth.

"Cheer up," he said. "Be happy. My power has won."

"What do you mean? Your power has won?" asked the puzzled Simanovitsch.

"I'm going today to Nicholas to tell him the truth."

"So what will that accomplish?"

"I shall predict the future. Call Papa up."

Simanovitsch rang the operator and put through the call. He got the palace operator.

"Where's the Tsar?" Rasputin demanded.

"He's with his ministers," came the reply.

"Well, call him. Tell him Rasputin calls."

In a few minutes, the Tsar's voice came over the line, "What is it, Father Grigori?" he said.

"I can't speak over the phone. Can I see you right away? It is urgent. Very urgent."

"Of course. Come right away."

When he arrived at the palace, Rasputin was ushered into a

meeting room, and Tsar Nicholas appeared in a few moments. Rasputin rushed over to him and embraced him in the Russian manner.

"Nicholas," he said, "last night I received the word of God. In three days you shall receive a telegram from your cousin Nicholas. It will say that the army has no more bread."

Then the peasant called for two glasses and a bottle of Madeira. He filled them both three-fourths full and handed one to Nicholas, and they both took a draught. Then Rasputin mixed the wine of the two glasses together and gave the Tsar his own glass and took the Tsar's glass. They both drained the remaining wine.

Rasputin conducted this ceremony in absolute silence. When they had done, he said, "Do not believe the telegram, Papa. There is plenty of bread. Nicholas has plans. He wishes to arouse a panic both in the army and back here in the government. Then he can call a retreat and march home to occupy the capital. He wants to declare himself the new Tsar, Papa. Do not let him."

Nicholas took this in with troubled eyes. It was true that his cousin wanted to be Tsar. And the situation at the front had deteriorated all through the long summer. He thanked Rasputin for his information and returned to the ministers' meeting.

Three days later, Nicholas received a telegram from Grand Duke Nicholas. It informed him of the depletion of all the food supplies and asked for his permission to call a retreat. The Tsar was shocked and decided to move. He informed his ministers, to their utter chagrin, that he was going to take over the Supreme Command of the Russian Armies and that he would be gone to the front within the week.

When Simanovitsch heard from Rasputin what had happened and that Nicholas had been delivered to the south, he could not contain himself.

"At last," he cried. "The Jews will begin to win their rights, at last! Rasputin, it is a miracle. We are saved."

"No, Simanovitsch, you are wrong," said the peasant. "It is no miracle. It is my power. Did I not tell you my power had conquered? When I desire that something should happen to help my cause, then it happens. But it is not a miracle. I do it myself. I have been born with this power."

Rasputin's claim that he possessed some wonderful cosmic force was supported by many events during the Tsar's reign. No one doubted that his highly charismatic presence could easily coerce people to do his bidding by mere suggestion, but many skoffed at him when he claimed for himself the power of prophesy. In one instance, these doubts caused an assassination.

That one instance occurred on a morning early in June 1911. The Tsar's impending trip to Kiev had been a topic of gossip for over a month now. While eating breakfast with Rasputin, Simanovitsch noticed that the peasant was especially excited about something. When he asked him what was wrong, Rasputin replied, "Listen to this, Aaron. A pogrom is about to break in Kiev. We must take measures."

"What's wrong down there?" asked Simanovitsch.

"When Prime Minister Stolypin goes with Nicholas, he will be shot by a Jew. They will arouse the people against them."

"Who will arouse them?"

"The police."

"Can't you persuade Nicholas to leave the Prime Minister behind?"

"No. This time he does not believe me. I can do nothing to save the Minister. Tell your people to beware."

When Nicholas went to Kiev later that week, Stolypin came along. A Jewish revolutionary named Bagrov shot Stolypin, just as Rasputin had predicted. The people wanted to lynch Bagrov and were incited to move against all the Jews.

Nicholas II didn't know quite what to do. If he stayed, he, too, risked the assassin's bullet. But if he left, all hell would surely break loose. He telegraphed Rasputin for advice, and received this answer:

JOY. REST. PEACE. YOU, THE FOUNDER OF GRACE AND PEACE STAND IN THE SHADOW OF NO ONE. THE BLOOD OF THE JEWS ON THE TSAR'S SOIL CRIES AS LOUDLY AS ANOTHER. REMAIN.

And so Nicholas remained in Kiev and saw to it that forceful measures were used to defeat the Jew-baiters.

But if skeptics still tenaciously doubted Rasputin's power of prophesy, only fools still denied his abilities as a healer. His most well-known case today is his cure of the Tsarevitch's hemophilia, but at that time very few people knew about either the heir's sickness or Rasputin's connection with it. The most popular and dramatic case of the day was the cure of Simanovitsch's second son.

Jacob Simanovitsch's right hand shook continually, and the left side of his body was completely paralyzed. The doctors all pronounced him incurable and he was resigned to a bedridden life. Simanovitsch had told Rasputin about his son many times, but for one reason or another, Rasputin put him off. Then one day, while visiting Simanovitsch at his own house, he spied the sixteen-year-old Jacob on the couch. He took pity on the young boy and told Simanovitsch to bring his son to his house tomorrow morning, before the dawn.

"Set him in the dining room," he said, "and leave before I arise."

Simanovitsch followed these orders and on his way out of Rasputin's house the next morning, after leaving his son in the dining room, he knocked on the monk's bedroom door to wake him up. Then he quickly left and went home to wait.

Rasputin emerged from his bedroom still smelling of a drinking party he had attended the previous night. His hair was tousled and flared out and his great gray bushy beard was ragged, spotted with bits of bread and cheese and matted with gravy. He went right up to where the boy sat and took him by the shoulders. He stared deeply into Jacob's eyes and shook him fiercely. Gradually Rasputin relaxed his hold on the frightened boy, and when Jacob had calmed down, the monk jumped up and shouted full-mouthed and hot-breathed into the little boy's face, "Get out of here you lazy lout, or I'll beat the young skin off your bones!"

The boy rushed out wildly and ran home as fast as he could. Not until he got safely inside his house did he realize what the awesome Rasputin had accomplished. Never before had he been able to use the left side of his body! Simanovitsch, with tears in his eyes, heard him recount what had happened. Jacob grew up to be as healthy as his father, and his symptoms never appeared again.

Nor was this the only salutary influence which Rasputin had over the Simanovitsch family. Simanovitsch himself enjoyed a sort of cure from his friend. His illness wasn't exactly a pathological condition; in fact, he himself considered it merely one of his more acceptable idiosyncrasies. He loved to gamble. In his earlier days before the war he had spent enormous amounts of time, money, and energy in the pursuit of Lady Luck. Since he won much more than he lost, he considered it to be at least a tolerable habit.

But once, after three days of fruitless search Rasputin found him hard at it at one of the tables of one of his innumerable clubs. Rasputin had an assignment for Simanovitsch to carry out, and the impatient peasant detested what he thought was a foolish waste of resources.

"Why have you spent the last three days in this foolishness?" asked the monk.

"But my friend, this isn't foolishness," Simanovitsch tried to explain. "I lost heavily last Wednesday evening—fifty thousand rubles—and I never leave a table until I regain my losses. How can you say that that is foolishness?"

"But, my fool, why do you play in the first place?" Rasputin shot back in exasperation. "You wouldn't have to win back your losses if you never played to begin with! You should spend your rubles to buy yourself a new brain, Simanovitsch. Not for the privilege of flipping over a piece of cardboard with numbers painted on it. Come. We shall have a drink."

He led Simanovitsch over to the bar, where they ordered two glasses of wine. Rasputin began to stare hard into his friend's now gaunt face. In silence, he repeated the strange ritual with the two wine glasses that he had performed with the Tsar. When they drained the glasses, Rasputin peered straight into his eyes. Simanovitsch felt a queer, disquieting sensation infuse him, and he acquiesced to the spell of those luminescent gray orbs.

"You will never gamble again," said Rasputin quietly. Then they went home. Until Rasputin died, Simanovitsch never again had the urge to engage in card games, play with the dice, wager on the roulette table, or even to play the horses. And even then his old passion never resurrected itself entirely, nor freed itself from the dampening specter of the monk's disapproval.

The Tsar fell under the sway of Rasputin's moral imperatives in a similar way. Nicholas II loved to drink. Some Court gossips said that he loved liquor more than anything else. True or not, we must acknowledge that anyone who wished to speak with Nicholas about serious business made the greatest efforts to see him before ten o'clock in the morning. Only then would he have any chance of speaking to a sober man.

The celebrations of Nicholas' palace regiments were notoriously outrageous, and when the Tsar honored them with his presence, they took on the appearance of orgies. The table was set with lush wines and meats, and salads and caviar graced the gullets of everyone, down to the last lusty wench.

Whenever Nicholas arrived at these banquets two officers were immediately put in charge of him. Their principal duties were to see to it that he arrived back at the palace safely. Usually they had to carry him home.

Rasputin acted equivocally in this matter. He at once scolded the Tsar and encouraged him. He would yell at him the morning after such a celebration, but they would spend the rest of the day joking about the events of the party and comparing notes. The Tsar listened to Rasputin's reprobations, but knew they would be followed by his questions: What did so-and-so do? Who did so-and-so get? How was this one? How was that dark-haired one? And thus the two cemented their working relationship.

When Nicholas went to the front, things changed only slightly. With the Tsar before his troops, Rasputin would tolerate no drunkenness. Although he invoked the legions of the Almighty to forbid the Tsar to drink, he knew it was hopeless to expect him to abstain absolutely. Besides, there were many favors to be gained by bargaining. So the men would bargain by telegraph. Rasputin would demand a month's sobriety, and Nicholas would bribe Rasputin with a ministerial appointment for two weeks off. Thus Nicholas stayed sober for two weeks at a time, and Rasputin built up a ministry favorable to his attitudes and those of his friend Simanovitsch.

EIGHT

Granted that Rasputin had a good relationship with Nicholas, how did he translate it into a working apparatus capable of fulfilling his needs and desires? He had, as all powerful men must, an organization. As the joke that traveled the rounds of Court society had it, the ladies made a ministry for Rasputin. Had the administrative senses of these wits been more acute, they would have realized the sad fact that in a comparison of the two ministries of the Tsar and of the peasant, the scales of objectivity, efficiency, and capability were all tipped in favor of Rasputin's side.

Old Countess Golovina, generally acclaimed the leader of this informal association of ladies, supported Rasputin both with her name and with her ancient authority at the summit of St. Petersburg society. Her daughter Munia acted as an intermediary between Rasputin and the upper echelons of the clerical dominions. Together these two devoted ladies informed Rasputin about the inner goings-on of these establishments and disseminated his attitudes and desires within their respective theaters of operation.

Vyrubova, the friend and only intimate of Alexandra, aided Rasputin in searching for candidates for his real ministry. Lydia Nikitina, a Court lady, took it upon herself to bridge the gap between Rasputin and the office of the Minister-President. The Vaskoboynikov sisters also pitched in. The elder one spent much time visiting the palace, so she informed Rasputin about the status of things there, giving him guest lists for banquets, schedules of Imperial activities, and similar information. Her younger sister, something of a flirt, knew hundreds of people of the "best sort." She kept tabs on the collective humor of these legions of the social elite, and saw to it that the peasant was informed.

To keep abreast of gossip, Rasputin leaned very heavily on the superb work of Akumina Laptinskaya, an omnipresent fixture of each and every social function of any importance. She continually amazed her friend with her display of secrets caught out of the very depths of people's private affairs. Unfortunately, the value of her work was diluted by the fact that she played with all the factions of an intrigue and so couldn't be trusted as an inviolate bearer of the truth.

One of the more beautiful and charming of the Court ladies—and also one of the most influential—was a German by birth. Mrs. von Dehn had married a Berliner who lived in Russia as an officer in the Russian Navy. These ties to Germany, naturally, disposed her to oppose the war. Since Rasputin was forever seeking ways to convince Nicholas II to sue for peace, she saw him as a kindred spirit and was endeared to him. They communicated frequently and copiously, but whenever they met face-to-face at a Court affair they feigned indifference to one another. Neither thought the connection an asset to his or her public image: Rasputin, because of his pacific spirit, shunned association with a German; Mrs. von Dehn, because of her impeccable social position, shunned association with peasants. This dissimulation notwithstanding, they got on famously.

Madame Kushina's beauty accummulated many trophies of praise, of which the most explicit was her nickname, "the beautiful one." Her social grace matched the charms of her exquisite visage, and an evening in her salon was refreshing after the noisy ostentation of the grosser affairs. Intimacy prevailed, with only selected members of the cream of society receiving her summons. Here Rasputin could talk freely with whomever he liked, for all were of his party. Indeed, most of his conversations with Mrs. von Dehn occurred on Kushina's plush sofas.

If Rasputin surrounded himself with many sources of information concerning the doings of the upper and middle classes, he did not neglect the world outside St. Petersburg. During his many earlier travels across the Russian continent he had observed much concerning the lives of the vast numbers of peasants and tradesmen. This store of information was continuously refreshed by Simanovitsch, who got word from his network of local correspondents. Thus Rasputin's perspective on Russian news was both deep and wide.

He needed this vast prospect, for he was always searching for men whom he could offer to Nicholas as candidates for appointment to one office or another. The job of filling vacancies, both in the ministerial council and in other, less glamorous institutions, was difficult. The Tsar dismissed his officers according to whim, and his whims were legion, as everyone knew. So if a man held a lower but more secure position—one, say, in the provinces out of the immediate sight of the Tsar—then he would show extreme reluctance to give it up for the very questionable advantages of a high-risk, high-pressure cabinet post. A high turnover rate combined with a high refusal rate to make life difficult for whomever was charged with supplying lists of prospective ministers and officials.

Nicholas, of course, called on many members of his Court to supply him with candidates, but most often the call went out to get Rasputin to the palace. Once, after such a summons, the Tsar told him, "Rasputin, I need a state secretary for the Interior Ministry. Minister Maklakov insists that the man must be a general. Who have we got?"

"Let me call home," replied Rasputin. He rang up his home phone and got Simanovitsch, whom he had just left, on the line. "Aaron, we need someone to be state secretary for Maklakov. A general, he says. Do you know anyone?"

"Wait a moment, Novitch. Let me think," came the immediate response. After a pause Simanovitsch continued, "No, I can't think of anybody. But my son Semion has come to see your nieces. Let me ask him."

Semion offered the name of Prince Volkonsky, the Vice President of the Duma. He wasn't a general, but Nicholas could get no other man to fill the post. So Prince Volkonsky was appointed.

Another time Nicholas asked Rasputin to fill a vacancy in the Holy Synod. Rasputin again went to his friend Simanovitsch, "We need a man to be Supreme Procurer for the Synod," he announced.

"How about old Raja?" replied Simanovitsch. "He's unassuming enough."

"He's that strange professor in the women's high school who wears those hideous wigs?"

"That's the one."

"How do you know him?" asked Rasputin.

"He's president of the Commercial Union."

"Is that one of your gambling clubs?"

"Now, Novitch, don't get angry—I told you I haven't been near those tables in months. But one must keep an eye on one's investment, mustn't one?"

And thus Professor Vladimir Raja was appointed Supreme Procurer of the Holy Synod.

For ministerial posts, positions of great power, more care went into the selection process. Before Rasputin proferred Stürmer's name as candidate for the Ministerial Presidency he and Simanovitsch had researched the backgrounds of many other possibilities. Stürmer was of Jewish lineage. His father, who made a fortune in the mining industry, had changed his name and converted to Orthodoxy so that he could receive a title. When Simanovitsch ascertained that Stürmer would not oppose his moves for equal rights for the Jews, he gladly sanctioned the candidate. Rasputin demanded that the candidates he preferred to Nicholas oppose the war as vehemently as he did himself. Stürmer's pacifism gained him the appointment.

When historians mention the power of Rasputin, primarily what they are referring to is his influence in having men appointed to positions of great power. He actually made very few of the day-to-day managerial decisions, but his real power lay in his ability to name the men who would make these decisions—and to influence them once they took office by holding threats and promises over their heads.

This all means that it is a difficult job to classify Rasputin. Was he a politician? He never held office. Was he a charlatan or quack? He cured a number of persons who were afflicted with what the medical profession claimed were incurable diseases. Was he a priest or a monk? He never took any vows or wore any sort of habit. Was he a peasant? He dined with royalty. Was he an entrepreneur? He never amassed any kind of wealth. In the end we must classify him as an amalgam of all of these, although strictly speaking he was none of them.

In passing judgment on Rasputin as a politician, we must recognize his great inadequacies. As a rough-nosed peasant, he didn't give the least care to his public image and, accordingly, his public image reflected gross distortions. When the average Russian heard the name of Rasputin, the picture which passed into his mind depicted a drunken, dirty *moujik*. All he knew was that a sordid peasant had somehow penetrated through the several layers of the Imperial society to the side of the Tsar, where he stood appointing and dismissing ministers, bishops, and generals, exerting mysterious force on the Imperial Family. They heard him named as the hero of too many scandalous stories and as the perpetrator of incredibly wild orgies at the Villa Rodé. Finally, he was touted and railed at as a hypnotist and magician.

Had the public been aware of Rasputin's relationship to the course of Alexis' illness, his beneficial effect on the humor of the Empress, and his ardent, fraternal support of the Tsar, perhaps they would have judged him less harshly. As it was, most men explained his presence at the Court by employing a conspiratorial theory: he was a subtly disguised foreign agent, they said, bent on the destruction of Mother Russia.

Again, we must remember that at a time when most men of public stature were cutthroats and buccaneers, this peasant Rasputin was a pacifist. His voice was probably the loudest raised against the insanity of the Great War. He pressed for immediate peace under any conditions, for he knew that Germany would benefit his country more if she were victorious and strong and could export her strength. He knew a weak, vanquished Germany had nothing to offer Russia but resentment and humbled pride.

When Nicholas appointed new ministers, he would say to them, "The only man in the world who merits my trust is Father Grigori. He is a messenger from God, a truly holy man. He is my confidant and I love him as a brother. Remember this."

One is tempted to let Rasputin's success get in the way of a true picture of his situation. If he could scold the Tsar of All the Russians; if he could command the support of that Tsar to the extent that the

Tsar claimed that he was the only man he could trust; if he could appoint and dismiss that Tsar's ministers, bishops, and generals, he did it all on the authority of his personal relationship to the Imperial Family. Personal relationships had been known to go sour in the past, and the consciousness of this possibility plagued the peasant throughout his career. Never for once did he believe that his status was secure or that the royal ground he trod on was firm. Wasn't Nicholas the most fickle ruler of recent times? But when Rasputin thought of the future, it was not to tremble and quaver at the prospect of death. He feared only his own downfall, for he knew that once his lifeline to the Tsar was cut, he would be washed into the vast ocean of Russian poverty and oblivion.

Looking at Rasputin in perspective, one is tempted to dismiss him as a bad influence on a weak monarch. But Rasputin was a sensitive, original humanist, who took Russia as it was and sought to improve on a working model. Toward the end of his life he prevailed on Nicholas to abandon his irrational prejudices. The Tsar ordered Interior Minister Protopopov to unearth from the archives the old portfolios which contained the writs against the Jews, instructing him to review the old laws on residence requirements in the cities. But the work was suspended before the people felt its fruits. It is the height of irony that the Tsar rescinded his support of this work out of his fear of revolutionaries, who assassinated Rasputin as a means to obtaining the liberation of the Russian people. Upon the monk's death, the Tsar ordered the ministries to cease work on all projects except the programs against the revolutionaries.

From his intimate position as manager, confidant, and secretary, Simanovitsch the Jew saw Rasputin displayed in his every mood, saw every hue and shade of his character. One night, long after Rasputin had been assassinated, Simanovitsch would write a letter to his grandson, who had challenged him in his association with "such a terrible creature as Rasputin." That letter provides an eloquent analysis of a misunderstood man:

> . . . under the mask. He had a strong spirit, stronger than the eagle which floats so proudly in the empyrean. He bent his

spirit to his designs by the sheer force of his will. Together, his spirit and will made him invincible.

He was a broad, ready-made man. A man grown in the wild—full of the passionate intensity of the Siberian wilderness. He was one of the few men in this world who travel on their own power, the source of life contained burning within their fiery souls. He was a brooder. His mind went swiftly over the trivial and bore down into the meat of intellectual fare. He reflected on all the problems of the government—and he wrought his own understanding of them, not some fifth-rate academician's version of abstract deficiencies or ideal possibilities. He wanted to see it work within his own lifetime—and he wanted to see it work within Nicholas' lifetime.

He continually sought to pierce into the core of reality to leave the husk to weaker souls. Twice he walked across the breadth of Russia and twice he walked south to the Holy Land and back again. He wandered greatly. And in his wanderings he observed. He watched the people of all the classes. He saw the farmer tilling his wheat, the shepherd tending his sheep. He saw the merchant peddling his cloth, and the fishmonger selling his fish. And his vision penetrated high into the chambers of the mighty. He talked with monks and with bishops, with farmers and with factory-owners and mine magnates. No class escaped his purview—he knew each life style. He stored all these impressions in his cavernous memory and he formed them into his unique philosophical character. His ideas were his own, and he infused them with his passion and created his own dream, cherishing its originality.

And where did this man come from? He came from the peasantry. He never forgot his brothers either. His deepest wish was to bring Nicholas to a consciousness of the plight of the Russian peasants. At the palace, with Nicholas, when the others talked about all the current religious and political issues, Rasputin talked always of the peasants. He regaled the Tsar with story after story of urgent needs and pathetic conditions. He stuck to one theme, and one theme only, the need for agrarian reform. "To free the peasants, to really free them, Nicholas," he would shout, "give them land. Without land a peasant cannot live." People would tell the Tsar: don't build the railroad into Siberia; it will corrupt the peasants; they will want more luxuries. Rasputin would grow furious when he heard this. "Luxuries!" he would shout, "why they don't even have enough tools to farm the land!"

And he told Nicholas of his dream, too. He wanted to see the establishment of a peasant monarchy. That was his dream— that Alexis inherit a peasant monarchy. He advised Nicholas to abolish the nobility and to redistribute state and monastic lands to the peasantry, especially to the veterans of the Great War. He urged Nicholas to take out a foreign loan to compensate the nobles for the expropriation of their land to the peasants. But forbid them to spend the money outside of Russia, he advised. Let them infuse the Russian economy. He was not a stupid rake. His schemes were well thought out.

During the war people charged that he was friendly to the enemy. But he just couldn't understand the business of warring on such a race as the Germans. He knew them from their colonies inside Russia. He had visited these and liked what he saw. The people and fields were clean, orderly, and solid. The colonies had huge economic potential, and the people knew how to tap it. Their tables were richly set; they had both tea and coffee. Besides, Germany sent Russia most of her agricultural machinery and iron tools. Why fight a country which had so much to offer in the line of hardware, technology, and example?

"All people are equal before God," he told the Tsar frequently. Always, one could hear him crying against regulations limiting the rights of the foreign peoples. Many orders to the detriment of our people were killed in the ministry before they got out. And many of the ministers who lost their jobs, lost them because they refused to dispense this peasant's mercy.

Many people say that this wasn't true; they say that Rasputin was a Jew-baiter and that I lowered myself by associating with him. Those are patent lies. He was no Jew-baiter. Yes, in the beginning he refused to help me with my petitions on behalf of the people. But he was surrounded then by people who were passionate, chronic Jew-baiters and anti-Semites. When I finally made him aware of the profundity of the persecution of our people he shed his coarse prejudices and aspired with me to redeem our people.

Many times we would argue the question. But mostly it would be a disagreement on priorities—not a clash of interests.

I would say, "'Rasputin, the concluding of peace is a very difficult matter. Let us throw all our energies into the Jewish question. If the Jewish problem is solved, we would get so much support from the American Jews that peace with Germany would be just a matter of time."

And Rasputin would answer, "Papa doesn't want peace. We can't have peace until Papa wants it. And during the war, he will hear nothing about equal rights for the Jews or for the foreign peoples. 'Give them a good constitution and they will call you Nicholas the Great,' I tell him. And he says that if he gives them a good constitution, his family will at least force his abdication and quite possibly take his life. He is very much afraid of ending up like that Serbian king, Alexander, you know. So we must end this war first, Simanovitsch. Then we can work for the rights."

And Rasputin was dedicated to this idea to the point that he risked his life for it. When it had become obvious that his enemies were growing bolder every day, I said to him, "Rasputin, I have this piece of property in the Holy Land, near Jerusalem. Give up this unhealthy and dangerous life here in St. Petersburg. You have done enough for your people. Leave the Court before your enemies gang up on you and lose their fears and kill you. Go, I will follow. We can spend our retirement there together, in peace."

And the peasant would say back to me, "Simanovitsch, I am glad that you plan to retire to the Holy Land. It would bring me much happiness to live out the rest of my life in the country where our Savior worked. But I must obtain this peace treaty first. I cannot go while the war ravishes the people."

Rasputin was also a good friend. One so rarely finds a good specimen of that creature in this modern world. He considered me (of all things!) a good mathematician, with a great experience of life and a solid practical understanding of the world. He trusted me and confided in me. I, too, felt dependent on him. I never experienced anything evil from my association with him; I never saw him do anything evil to another. Certainly he was gross. Certainly he insulted many great ladies and stuffy gentlemen. But I salute his demeaning of these people. It was the only source of humility in their lives. Besides, I do not count the presence or absence of social niceties among the evils of the world.

He bore no guilt for the fact that Nicholas was a weak man. Through my mediation he helped thousands of people, and with his influence and my wealth we saved many from poverty, death, humiliation, and persecution. I shall never forget this about Rasputin—and I hope that you and the younger people of the world never forget it either. I have no right either to condemn him or even, in general, to judge him. There are no people without weaknesses, but in my view Rasputin was more honorable than all the people who gathered in his home.

The letter goes on, but we can leave off here. Simanovitsch tended to repeat himself when writing letters, and we already have a good picture of the real Rasputin. He was first a monarchist; second, a sensualist; third, a friend and humanist; and only fourth, a politician.

NINE

Regardless of historical opinion, Rasputin was a figure one had to deal with to achieve a career at the summit of Tsarist Russia. Each man dealt with him in his own way. Some, whose fear balanced their hate, avoided contact with him. Others actively sought him out. A few wanted to meet him as a friend; more often they wanted him as an advocate for their cause; but most frequently of all, they came to confront him as an enemy.

One pale cold day as Rasputin was entering his home at the end of a long business day, Simanovitsch found the card of Count Serge Witte in the silver plate on the hall table. On the back of the card the Count had hurriedly written,

> Dear Aaron,
>   Please call me at my home. I have some urgent business I wish to discuss with you immediately,
>
> Signed,
> Count Witte

Even though he was dead tired, Simanovitsch called up the Count and made an appointment to meet him at his home later in the evening. The Count's secretive manner piqued his curiosity, which counterbalanced the demands of his weary bones. He dined at eight, as was his custom, and afterward drove over to the Count's house to keep his ten o'clock appointment.

When they had made their salutations and exchanged their

pleasantries and after the servants had served the brandy and departed, the Count looked over at Simanovitsch, paused dramatically, and then began, "Aaron Simanovitsch, can I have your promise that the conversation we are about to have will remain absolutely confidential? That it shall never, even in the slightest allusions, leave this room?"

"My dear Count," Simanovitsch answered, "I do not know the purpose of this little engagement of ours; but I can see that you are highly excited by the burden of your knowledge and desires. Therefore, I give you my word—never shall I even allude to this conversation."

Count Witte sighed a breath of relief. "Now, then. I have requested you to come here this evening because I wanted you to hear my plan for the betterment of the Jewish conditions. They are bad off, eh? I want to speak to you because I know that you take these conditions to heart, n'est-ce pas? You feel badly that your people suffer so much degradation and poverty . . . "

"What is your plan, Count Witte?" interrupted Simanovitsch, who was tired and feeling a headache coming on from the snifter of good, stiff Russian brandy.

"My plan is this," resumed Witte, quite unperturbed. "I shall win back my old position of power in the Tsar's government. From a seat on the ministry, I can press forward your fine work in behalf of your people. But to get back to my position—this, my good friend, will necessitate your helping me. I need you to introduce me to Rasputin, I need you to speak to him about me—to talk me up to him."

Here the Count paused to ascertain what effect his proposition had produced in Simanovitsch. But he was ill rewarded by the bland countenance of the Jew. Simanovitsch had often been confronted by people in high positions who desired him to introduce them to Rasputin. His expression reflected neither surprise nor disdain, so Witte went on.

"You seem not to be very surprised, Simanovitsch. Perhaps you already guessed my purpose, eh? What do you think of my plan?"

Simanovitsch hemmed and then brought out quickly, "Count

Witte, if you win back your old position of power, do you give me your word that you will help me?"

"Yes, on my word," replied the Count.

"Then I shall help. But we cannot count on my work alone. Your wife, the Countess, has many poor people coming to her kitchens seeking meals and jobs. Rasputin sends many of these beggars there. Make sure, Count Witte, that your wife treats these poverty-stricken people with tenderness and care, for they report back to him."

"Yes, yes, I shall see to that. But, Simanovitsch," returned Witte, "I have been wondering—don't you think that Rasputin would favor me more readily if I approached him as a strange man, that is, if I took a disguise? Then he would not have to forget all these old associations which go with the name of Witte."

"That's a good idea, Count Witte," said our friend. "When you appear at Rasputin's home for his dinners, I shall speak of you as Ivan Feodorovitch. You will be more discrete incognito."

But the Count's dissimilation didn't last long under the pressure of Rasputin's scrutiny. When Simanovitsch had drawn his friend's attention to the person of Ivan Feodorovitch and then later talked freely about this person's virtues, Rasputin smiled broadly and said, "My friend, you do not deceive me in the least. Your Ivan Feodorovitch is none other than old Count Witte come begging for my protection. Really, I am flattered. It shall be. He can help us in our cause. Set up a meeting for him. But it must not be here. It would not be wise for us to be seen together. The Dowager Empress Maria Feodorovna would suspect some intrigue against her. We must avoid her agents. I leave the place up to you."

Simanovitsch had a friend in the jewelry business, Chaiyat, who owned a small villa about twenty miles outside of the capital. Simanovitsch arranged to get the use of Chaiyat's villa for the meeting. After he picked up the keys for the place from his friend he sent them to Witte with instructions which told him how to get to the place, what time to arrive, and what to say to the soldier Simanovitsch had hired to guard the grounds. The meeting occurred at four o'clock on a Saturday afternoon in spring. When Rasputin arrived, Witte was already there.

Rasputin opened their little talk by saying, "Serge Yulievitch, you have a title; what does it mean?"

Witte replied, "It means, 'little Count,' Rasputin. I bought it."

"What do you want of me, little Count?" purred Rasputin.

"My dear sir, when I fell from the ministry the war still seemed a glorious and adventuresome road for our nation. My opposition to the war caused my disgrace."

"My dear sir," Rasputin interrupted, "you should not have fallen into disgrace because you opposed this horrible war. You should be kissed! I, too, hate it. I tell Nicholas every day to get it over with. But Papa loves the war. He enjoys the big military hullabaloo. But the parade has turned into a ghastly mess. I will help you. I shall tell Nicholas to let you end the war for him. I shall say to him that you can be trusted. We shall see what can be done."

Elated with these words of support from Rasputin, Count Witte developed his theme, "Rasputin, the newspaper *Novoye Vremya* daily disgorges volleys of propaganda which whip up the people for war. We must put an end to this if our cause is to succeed."

"You are quite right, Witte, that paper must go. They have taken potshots at me. Take care of it. You should buy it and turn it to our side."

"I shall do what I can," said Witte.

Within the next few weeks, Rasputin found occasion to approach Nicholas on the subject of Witte. He began by descanting the wonderful work which his wife, Madame Mathilde, was doing for the petitioners whom he sent to her kitchens. Then he reported to his Imperial friend the salient points of his conversation with the Count. Finally, he exhorted the Tsar to rely on Witte and appoint him to the post of Minister-President.

Out of fear, however, Nicholas rejected Rasputin's advice. The image of the murdered King and Queen of Serbia still haunted his dreams. He knew his relatives favored the war. Why his cousin, Grand Duke Nicholas, had never been more fulfilled than now, leading the great Russian standard across the fields of Eastern Europe. The Tsar knew that the Old Court would only interpret Witte's appointment as an unannounced move to end the war, and he believed that they wouldn't stand for it.

Meanwhile, Witte informed Simanovitsch of a talk he had had with the editor of the *Novoye Vremya*. This man had disclosed the hapless state of the paper's finances and requested Witte to advise him how to pull the dying organization out of an inevitable fiscal collapse.

"In short," Witte summarized, "he wants to sell, and he wants me to get permission from Finance Minister Bark to allow him to sell. Can you get up the money, Simanovitsch?"

Simanovitsch put Witte off for the time being, telling him he had to speak to Rasputin first. A few days later he reported the substance of this meeting to the peasant and asked for instructions.

"Let your clever bankers buy it, Simanovitsch," Rasputin told him. "They will be the ones who will benefit most from a change in the laws. Tell them that they must do their part."

So Simanovitsch went to his friends, the banker Dimitri Rubinstein, and the entrepreneurs, Moses Ginsberg and Baron Ginsburg. They were pleased when Simanovitsch informed them of Rasputin's support of the venture, and together with Witte they purchased the stock of the anti-Semitic periodical. When in the course of this transaction they realized the nature of Simanovitsch's tight ties to Rasputin, they marveled and exhorted their compatriot to bring the peasant even closer to the cause of the Jews.

During these operations, the Old Court also got wind of Count Witte's growing friendship with Rasputin. Simanovitsch had taken the best precautions to camouflage this affiliation, but the pervasive espionage agency which the Old Court had developed through years of experience pierced the subterfuge. In the light of exposure, Witte's cause stood little chance of maturing. Yet he never gave up hope of regaining his old position, and neither did he relinquish his friendship with Rasputin. The newspapers listed the cause of his death in March of 1915 as coronary failure. But those more keenly attuned to the clandestine workings of the nation cast a righteous eye in the direction of the Old Court and whispered over their shoulders to their neighbors, "Poison."

Some months after the news of Witte's death had broken, Simanovitsch confronted Rasputin over breakfast. Rasputin had just returned the previous night from a visit to Tsarskoye Selo and the Jew picked up signs of excitement from the peasant's demeanor.

"What's wrong?" he queried.

"I can't divulge it; it's secret," said Rasputin.

"That's all right, I can keep a secret. What went wrong at the palace last night?" insisted Simanovitsch.

"Simanovitsch, do not breathe a word of this, not a hint to anyone. Alexandra is in a state of shock. She is beating her head against the walls and crying a flood over the stupidity of Nicholas. He really did it this time, Aaron. Lord Kitchener—he's a big English general—was sailing to Russia on a British ship to help us end the war quickly. Nicholas let the news break. The Germans found out about it; they sunk the ship. Now the English blame us for it. All England's up in arms against us."

"But why is Alexandra so disturbed at this?" asked Simanovitsch. "It will smooth over soon enough."

"No, Simanovitsch. You were up late again last night, eh? You're not thinking. Who should the suspicion of the people fall upon? Our German-born Empress, eh? They will say that she is the one who gave the information to the Germans."

"How did Nicholas let it out then? Do you know?"

"At first he claimed he had told no one about it. But later when I talked to him alone, I found out that he got the telegram, telling him when the general would arrive, early in the morning. Then later on, when he had breakfast with the Palace Commander Voyeikov and Admiral Nilov, after a few bottles of wine with his eggs—do you see?—he let it out that the war would soon be over because he had a big English general coming on Thursday. That bastard Voyeikov went scuttling off to Prince Nicholas Andronnikov, who sent words to his friends in Berlin."

"Rasputin, it would be good for Russia if she could get rid of that man Andronnikov. He causes much trouble," replied Simanovitsch.

"My friend, Andronnikov is only a big bubble. He will burst one day and stink strongly."

Rasputin's metaphor misinformed his friend. Andronnikov wasn't merely a bubble, but the center of a well-organized spy network which systematically shunted information from Russia to Germany by way of Sweden. He resembled a bubble only in shape, being inordinately corpulent. But in spite of his obesity, he moved with agility and was quite active.

Very little was known about Prince Andronnikov's background. But he compensated for this obscurity by bridging business contacts with almost everyone in the Court and society. Although he professed the Lutheran faith, he corresponded frequently with the high clergy of the Orthodox Church. Besides very publicly making friends with many of these prelates, he cultivated the habit of sending holy cards along with his letters to all his acquaintances and friends. Not infrequently Alexandra would receive an icon he had sent by post. The gullible were taken in by these habits, and Andronnikov earned the reputation of being a very holy and pious man.

Before the war, however, he had balanced this image with the image of a dapper man-about-town. He was a bachelor, and many women enjoyed his hospitality. People said that he was something of a skirt-chaser, but they smiled when they said it—for they knew he took the sacraments regularly. Indeed, hadn't his own cousin, Princess Orbeliani, introduced him to the Court?

Still another aspect of Andronnikov's unctuous personality surfaced during the war. His home was always crowded with young people; most of them were new, handsome officers. He offered them food, drink, and hospitality—and money, if they got into trouble. They had been torn away from their farms and out of their villages; they had been shipped out of the only familiar regions of their lives. His place became a haven for them, for they were mere boys, frightened of the strange, huge city, and in need of the paternal comfort he extended to them.

Most wartime armies spawn homosexual associations; the Russian army was no different. Andronnikov simply took advantage of the anxieties of these young men's unnatural environment and turned it into profit, learning much free military information he could pass on—for a price—to the Germans. It was a perverse kind of economy.

By anyone's standards, Prince Andronnikov himself was sick. The fact of his treason contributed to his decadence. But the greatest measure of his soul was the depths of ignominy to which he sunk in engineering the frame-up and trial of his loyal friend, Dumbadze.

Dumbadze was a cousin of Prince Andronnikov, related to him through his father. Along with his friend, an engineer named Veller, he worked in the War Ministry, then headed by Sukhomlinov, a friend of the Prince. Since the first moment he set eyes on the youthful Veller, Andronnikov wanted him and, through Sukhomlinov, he invited the pair to one of his notorious parties. Dumbadze and Veller civilly refused the invitation, claiming previous engagements. When Sukhomlinov informed the Prince, he flew into a rage, shouting, "They refuse to dine at my tables, eh? They are too good to accept the invitation of Andronnikov, is that it? Above my hospitality! Ha! We shall see, Sukhomlinov, how high they float when I get through with them."

Sukhomlinov witnessed this display of passionate vanity with feelings of trepidation. He knew the lengths that Andronnikov would go to satisfy his ego. He decided to send the two off to America to purchase munitions, hoping that the Prince would cool off in the interim.

When they returned, however, Andronnikov denounced them as spies. Within the week they returned, he had them arrested, imprisoned, and brought before a military court, stacked with men he controlled. It sentenced them to death by hanging and stipulated that the sentence be executed within forty-eight hours.

The relatives of the two men sought out Simanovitsch and pleaded for justice. He reported the case to Rasputin, and Rasputin, in turn, obtained pardons from Nicholas.

Prince Andronnikov held too much power, and acted with too much stealth to enable anyone to expose him. Nevertheless, one evening Rasputin spied him among his dinner guests and lit into him. He jumped onto a chair and shouted, "You, Andronnikov, you fat, filthy pig—you are a swine. I will not have hogs at my table. You are filthy; you have blood on your paws! You feed the ocean's fish with human blood. It is you who spilled the blood of Kitchener. It is you who turned in your own friends to the secret police. Your flesh stinks with its sins. Get out of my house! Don't ever let me catch even a whiff of your pig odor in these rooms or I shall throw you onto the fire and drown you in your melting blubber, you blood-pawed swine. Get out, get out, get out!"

The infuriated peasant leaped down off the chair, rushed at the fat man, screeching obscenities at him, and chased him out of his house. After news of this public scolding had spread around the circles of St. Petersburg, people began to avoid the corpulent Prince, and his power gradually diminished. One day it was snuffed out altogether; one of his abandoned lovers poisoned him.

It wasn't always, though, that Rasputin allowed his enemies to escape his wrath merely with tongue-lashing and ostracism. In most cases he actively sought to cut them down from whatever position they were sniping at him. One such hapless enemy was Interior Minister Maklakov. Maklakov had obtained his position by dint of his extraordinary powers for successful flattery. His charms worked wonderfully on the incredulous Tsar and his family, but he gauged his position falsely when he took it upon himself to insult Sima-novitsch, and through him, Rasputin.

At House 14, Fontanka Prospect, the glow of a thousand glittering party lights burst through the windows and reflected onto the snow-covered street below. The light disclosed a procession, as magnificent carriage after magnificent carriage disgorged its bejew-eled and bedecked passengers. A vermilion carpet led these cele-brants into the din and dazzle of the nocturnal festivities attending the opening of one of Simanovitsch's clubs. Had one been able to peruse a list of the guests invited to the affair, one could have been able to pick out such luminous names as Count Leo Tolstoi, Baron Adrien Roop, Lieutenant Vladimir Bermand, Prince Bermand-Avalov, Count Musvitz Shadorsky, and Jacob Rosen.

The club's specialty was lotto, a game played much like modern-day Bingo, but for immensely higher stakes. Mostly, though, the club was simply a place where those sharing the beliefs, disposi-tions, and financial resources of men like Simanovitsch could go to enjoy an evening of convivial, fraternal society. Now and then the officers of the club organized dinners and concerts. Sometimes Rasputin was invited as a sort of insurance, among other things. He never gambled, but he attended when he heard that he could meet certain of his friends whose company especially pleased him.

The average fare of the club teetered on the luxurious. When word arrived that Rasputin was on his way, the culinary efforts were doubled, the Imperial wine cellar was ransacked for its most exquisite ports, and an automobile of the political police was fitted up with a spare load of wines, in case Rasputin suddenly decided to bring the party somewhere else.

One day Maklakov called one of his inferiors, a man called Nikoladja, into his office and deputized him as a special assistant to the Interior Minister. He charged him with the task of mounting what he was pleased to call a "revision" of the club's license. It amounted to an executive order closing the club down. Nikoladja, however, numbered in the ranks of Simanovitsch's legions and accordingly sent notice of the impending action to his superior.

Simanovitsch called an emergency meeting of the club's elected officers. They decided that the information must have been false, that Nikoladja must have been misled. Their procurer, Jacob Rosen, was judicial advisor to the powerful and reactionary Union of the Arch-Angel Michael, and they were sure that Maklakov wouldn't dare take action against them. So they decided to let things stand as they were.

Two days later their president, Baron Roop, received a letter from the city licensing bureau, informing him that the club's license would be prematurely expired by executive decree in two days. Maklakov had dared.

A second emergency session was convened. This time the concensus favored an appeal to Rasputin; naturally, Simanovitsch received the honor of approaching him with their plea.

Simanovitsch picked up the phone and dialed his friend. "Rasputin," he said when the connection was made, "I have just received word from the boys at Fontanka that they are being closed down by the city on account of you."

"Those bastards," sputtered Rasputin. "Who is it, Simanovitsch?"

"Well, the letter is from the Director of Licensing, a fellow called Drachuvsky."

"Drachuvsky, Licensing Bureau. Okay, Simanovitsch, tell your friends not to worry," Rasputin said, hanging up.

Simanovitsch replaced the phone, grinning from ear to ear. "I just feel sorry for the Drachuvsky," he thought; "I don't think he knows what he's got himself into."

Rasputin rang Drachuvsky immediately.

"Director Drachuvsky?"

"Yes."

"This is Rasputin. You are a blackguard, a pimp, a foul stinking dog. Why did you send that letter to Baron Roop? Why, don't you know that that's the only place left where I can amuse myself in this stuffy town? How dare you revoke their license! Do you want to be giving out fish licenses in Siberia, fool? You shall change your order immediately."

"But, but . . . ," stammered the director, who had had no idea of whom he had been playing with at the time he sent the letter. "I didn't know a thing about it! It was all on orders. I didn't have a thing to say about it. Maklakov sent down this letter. 'Close that stinking peasant's nest,' he said. 'I shall have no more of his blasphemous orgies while I'm Interior Minister!' The Minister holds much power, Father Grigori. One has to obey his order, or . . . " And here the whining, terrified subordinate collapsed in tearful trepidation and confusion.

The director's words set Rasputin into a steaming rage. "Powerful?" he screamed to his nieces as he stomped around the room. (The phone had already bounced off the wall.) "Stinking nest is it? Blasphemous orgies, are they?" And here he staggered into his workroom to compose his sentiments in his pelucid prose:

Hear me, Minister Maklakov. You believe that you can do anything you want because Papa brought you out of Chernigov. He liked your long mustache, Minister. And he liked your jokes—but your mustache is all puffed out of proportion now, Minister Maklakov. And your jokes are flat. I am going to pull out your hairs from your lip, you fat-tongued, red-nosed clown. How dare you even think you can close my club? Are you crazy? Thank God and Father Grigori that you do not find your bowl-bellied carcase in Siberia. I am satisfied with firing you. You are a fool, Maklakov, and you will always be a fool. Complain about me if you dare. I spit on your name.

Grigori

A large splotch blurred the opening of this epistle when Maklakov received it. Apparently, Rasputin felt compelled by his rage to invest his last statement with literal meaning. In any case, the Minister lost his post that same week.

It had not been long after Rasputin entered the larger society of St. Petersburg that he encountered a much more serious threat. The stimulus that initiated the roundabout plot against his life arose from the resentment of the evaporated expectations of two pompous Court ladies and mutual friends, the Countess Kleinmichel and the Countess Ignatieva.

Countess Kleinmichel's salon was distinguished by the attendance of many important Court dignitaries. Ambassadors, consuls, attachés, ministers, governors, state secretaries, bankers, mine-owners, industrial magnates, admirals, generals, colonels, counts, dukes, princes, and crowds of ladies swept through her rooms in a heavy tide of glitter, glamour, and rustling elegance. She presented herself extremely well and possessed a reputation for prodigal hospitality; in fact her salon was a regular stopover on the agenda of many visiting statesmen.

When Rasputin began appearing at high social gatherings, she naturally extended herself and her fare to the *starets*. She and her confidante, Countess Ignatieva, culled his friendship in the hopes of thus building a direct bridge to the fountain of high society, the Imperial seat. But Rasputin, as we have already seen, had an acute vision and an overriding will. When the two ladies perceived that they just couldn't put anything over on him or add him to their guests as a lure for Imperial consideration, they reacted sharply.

A young, zealous monk named Iliodor became their instrument of revenge. The monk was bent on reforming the Orthodox Church, hoping to rejuvenate the dying, traditional fervor of the clergy and to cleanse these ranks of their impurity and irreverence. At first, he became a friend of Rasputin, but it didn't take much to convince him of the error of his friendship. These ladies provided that measure of persuasion.

Rasputin heard the first faint murmurings of the hue and cry which Iliodor unleashed while he was visiting Praskovia in Pokrovskoye. Bishop Barnabas traveled from St. Petersburg with the news of the impending maelstrom and exhorted the peasant to return with him immediately to meet the tempest and quell the protests. He offered to set up a meeting between Rasputin and Khvostov, Governor of Nizhni Novgorod and friend to the infuriated zealot. Governor Khvostov had let Barnabas know that he felt the next most appropriate step in his career was a promotion from governor to Interior Minister. At the same time, Khvostov claimed to be the one from whom Iliodor received his cues, and that for a sufficient boost—say to the already-mentioned post—he would quiet the young monk down.

Rasputin agreed with the Bishop's analysis: action had to be taken immediately. In a matter of days he embarked with his clerical friend on a steamer on the Volga. At the landing they were met by Khvostov, whom the bishop had previously telegrammed. They set out to find a suitable inn where they could procure lunch and hash out the terms of the agreement.

Rasputin first questioned Khvostov about his alleged membership in the reactionary Union of the Russian People. When Khvostov assured him that he had never belonged to the association but had to support their monarchistic ideals, Rasputin was satisfied.

"And if I secure your appointment to the post, can you assure me of your effectiveness in putting down this madman?" he said.

"Iliodor takes his orders from me," answered Khvostov. "If he knows I am against him, he will cease."

"And if I order you to exile him," persisted Rasputin, "Will you do that?"

"When he finds out that I am no longer in support of him, then he will disappear of his own accord."

"In that case," finished Rasputin, "it shall be done."

Rasputin talked to Tsar Nicholas about it; Khvostov got the job and Iliodor the boot. But the thrust which sent him away was delicately administered and the trajectory handsomely planned. Khvostov packed Iliodor off to Oslo, Norway, furnishing him with twenty-thousand rubles to tide him over the interruption of their affiliation. Soon after his arrival in Sweden, he and Khvostov resumed their correspondence via special messenger and exchanged thoughts concerning the fine details of a plan to assassinate Rasputin.

Fortune smiled upon Rasputin in the body of Anton Belletsky, assistant to the Interior Minister. He yearned for Khvostov's office and worked each day under the tension of this desire. To relieve this tension he noted each and every act of his superior and recorded it in a journal. Besides this, he snooped around trying to get something on him. Working in this direction, he came upon Khvostov's special correspondence with Iliodor via the young journalist-turned-messenger, Rashevsky. He stole one of the letters from the careless youth, discovered the plot, and persuaded Rashevsky to work with him in exposing the conspiracy. In fact, he encouraged him to report to Simanovitsch and disclose one of the damning letters.

Rashevsky approached Simanovitsch, telling him for whom he worked, and what his job consisted of. He told him that he was on his way at that moment to deliver a bag of letters to Iliodor in Oslo, and offered Simanovitsch the perusal of a letter. This accomplished, the two brought the affair to Rasputin.

Naturally the letter galvanized Rasputin, and they discussed the most effective counteraction for them to take. Simanovitsch considered it appropriate to place the burden of exposing the plot on a disinterested party; it was bound to cause greater sympathy that way. Rasputin agreed, asking Simanovitsch to contact Army General Belyayev. The following day, he called on the officer at the army offices.

"Why do you come to me with this information, Simanovitsch?" the general asked after he had listened to the Jew's report. "What have I to do with some crazy monk in Norway?"

"We wish that an investigation be made into the affair," answered Simanovitsch. "We believe you are the man best qualified by temperament and reputation to undertake the inquiry. It would be rendering a great service to Papa, General Belyayev. The Tsar holds much affection for his *starets*."

"How much affection, Simanovitsch?" the general queried.

"Whatever amount you wish to be shown, General."

"An appointment to the War Ministry, as Minister."

"Of course."

From this point on, Rashevsky, Belletsky, and General Belyayev worked together on the case. Rashevsky was dispatched to Norway to deliver the letters as scheduled. He was searched at the border by military agents of the General. They recorded the substance of the letters, photographing some of the most salient. Rashevsky had been briefed beforehand and continued quietly on to Oslo after the search. On the return trip, this time carrying the prose of Iliodor, he again acceded to the surveillance of the military spies. He finished the trip in Khvostov's office, handing him the leather satchel on time, thus averting any suspicion.

One of the letters of this batch named three peasants from Tsaritsyn as the assassins. It informed the Interior Minister (and the spying General Belyayev) of their readiness to execute the plan. They only awaited the word from Khvostov.

General Belyayev acted swiftly and had the three peasants arrested. Later Rasputin intervened on their behalf and the General allowed their release. When Khvostov heard of their arrest he knew the plot had been discovered and disavowed any and all affiliation with the thugs. As Tsar Nicholas was at the front at the time, no action was taken against him.

At this point Khvostov made a serious mistake. Knowing Simanovitsch's part in the exposure of his conspiracy, he planned to frame Simanovitsch on charges of espionage in order to do away with what he considered a meddlesome Jew. To effect his vengeance, he ordered his agents to search the Jew's house. Papers were collected along with Simanovitsch himself, who was thrown into solitary confinement.

For sixteen days no one knew of his whereabouts. Finally his son Semion learned from a fellow law student that a case was being prepared by the Interior Ministry against a certain important Jew.

Putting two and two together, he brought the news to the Empress Alexandra that his father had been arrested.

The Empress was bowled over. "It is a revolution!" she exclaimed. "Khvostov has acted against the Tsar!" She immediately telephoned Stürmer, the Minister-President.

He was stunned. "Why, the brazen man!" he exclaimed. "Are any of us safe anymore from his 'efficiency'?"

When Stürmer informed Rasputin, he hit the roof. "He's done what?" he uttered, unable to take in the audacity of the feat the first time. "Arrested? For spying? On his way to Siberia? Why that bile-blooded bastard. How in the name of Mother Russia did I get him his job? Yes. Thank you, Minister Stürmer. I shall go immediately to headquarters. See what you can do about his family. I shall return soon."

Rasputin drove all night in a police vehicle, reaching Nicholas at the front at dawn. Here he told him the incredible story and persuaded him to return with him that same day.

Khvostov was ready for the Tsar's summons, however. During the entire interview he pleaded most cunningly for his case. He laid all blame for the conspiracy against Rasputin on the shoulders of his assistants, Rashevsky and Belletsky. He even took for himself the credit for exposing the plot. As for Simanovitsch, he asseverated his contention that the man was definitely a foreign agent, and presented the whole of his fraudulent case against him.

Throughout the course of this two-hour interview, Nicholas exuded his famous amiability. Smiling and nodding, encouraging and questioning, he drew out the whole of Khvostov's apology. When it was over he thanked the Minister for his time and consideration in making this evening appointment. Khvostov left at nine o'clock at night.

As he crossed the palace grounds the Minister was invigorated by the crisp winter air. The bushes bent low with their burden of January snow, and Khvostov may have fancied he was seeing Nature bowing to the superiority of his genius. Upon his arrival home he picked up a letter which had been delivered by special messenger while he had been out. It read in part,

—Therefore, consider it your fortune to receive the following: immediate and total relief from any and all duties and responsibilities incumbent upon you as Interior Minister; immediate and irrevocable suspension of all title, honors, privileges, special considerations, and remunerations devolving upon an officer of the Tsar's Ministry—

Nicholas II, Tsar of Russia

Khvostov reeled. He couldn't believe it. He just couldn't believe it. He stumbled into his study and put down several quick brandies that only partially quelled the revulsion in his stomach. His world tottered about him; he was in ruin.

When he regained consciousness about half an hour later, he retrieved his hat, scarf, gloves, and overcoat from the servants and had his carriage called around again. For the second time that evening he made the fifteen-mile trip to Tsarskoye Selo in the cold brittle night under the outstretched, twinkling stars. When his carriage finally rolled up to the gate he barked his peremptory orders to the gate-keepers and then received the final twist of the knife: the Imperial gates would no longer open for Khvostov. He took one last look at the glimmering shadows of the palace buildings beyond, saluted, and settled back for the long ride over the bumpy, frozen roads.

Later that night Stürmer rang up Khvostov. The latter's voice came through the line in a whisper, in a defeated monotone. Stürmer informed him that he was banished from the capital, that he was to prepare himself for exile to Siberia. They would come for him in the morning. There was no response—just the faint click of a receiver gently falling on a phone-box, cutting the last connection with the grand world of the Imperial Court.

Belletsky received a specially created office—assistant to the Minister of Police—prepatory to his appointment to the Interior Ministry. General Belyayev received appointment as War Minister. Of course, Simanovitsch returned from Tver, his furthest penetration into Siberia, making this triumphant trip surrounded by his ten bodyguards. At his instigation, a thorough search of Khvostov's house was undertaken. The documents retrieved revealed the collusion of Khvostov with all manner of sordid Jew-baiters and organized anti-Semites. The material was given to Prince Golalvani, a delegate to the Duma. Eventually it found its way into Alexander Kerensky's hands, whence it became public and dissolved what was left of the reputation of the would-be assassin.

TEN

Rasputin engaged in battles with many men for many different reasons, but none of his struggles counted for more than the ones on behalf of the Jews. As we have already seen, it took him a while to warm up to the cause. But when he did, he gave it the healthy, invigorating benefit of his remarkable energy. Up to this time, these activities had been mostly piecemeal efforts aimed at alleviating specific problems. The major instrument he used was the petition to Nicholas, a legal document pleading for a reversal of an already existing executive or judicial decree (the two adjectives were synonomous in Tsarist Russia, signifying the same source).

When Simanovitsch was exiled to Siberia, the Jewish community shuddered in fear. Wave after wave of agitation spread through every street of every ghetto. But when he returned victorious, the cheers resounded even into the outlying homes of the more fortunate gentiles. His procession back from Tver weaved its way through ranks of happy tradesmen, merchants, butchers, grocers, and peddlers of all kinds. His sudden victory over Khvostov transformed what had been a terrific fervor into ardent accolade and reverential exhortation.

Trying to make use of this groundswell of emotion, Simanovitsch decided to call together a number of prominent men to discuss ways and means of advancing Jewish rights on the crest of this wave of sentiment. Attending this conference were Rasputin, Minister-President Stürmer, Metropolitan Bishop Pitirim, and Bishop Isidor.

The men gathered together in the Alexander Nevsky Monastery.

The meeting began in the evening, in the high-ceilinged private dining room of Bishop Pitirim. The men talked casually and informally about the general situation. At one point Simanovitsch proposed that Stürmer do some spade work to see if he could establish a concerted ministerial position on behalf of the Jews. Stürmer replied at length:

"Simanovitsch, we are all aware of your anxiousness to get the movement going. Your intentions are superb. Your strategy, on the other hand, is not. Don't you realize, Simanovitsch, that neither I nor any member of the ministry can do anything at all about the Jewish laws unless Nicholas so directs us? Wait a moment. I know what you are going to say. Yes, the former Tsar's ministers all took independent courses and actions, if such courses suited them. But that was different; the Tsars were different. Does anyone know better than you how many times Nicholas has allowed his displeasure to sever his relationship with a minister? Even I do not trust him. Why, he may cast me off this very night if he hears a story about me which nettles him. If I took any sort of initiative in this matter, even such an innocuous one as you suggest, I would forfeit my career. No, Simanovitsch. Nicholas must be your target. It is you who must take the initiative, and it is we who must follow. You must talk to the Tsar."

Everyone, including Simanovitsch himself, recognized the truth in this speech. Bishop Pitirim later took up the point that Simanovitsch should speak to Nicholas.

"Tomorrow, Simanovitsch," he said, "Rasputin and I are going to attend the church service at Tsarskoye Selo. You should come with us. After the Mass, the Empress has arranged for us to luncheon with some wounded men from her hospital. I hear that the hospital needs certain supplies like cognac, tea, sugar, marmalade, and the like. I have a complete list in my room—wait, I'll send for it." The bishop charged the attending monk with the task and continued. "You should bring these supplies, Simanovitsch, and I will make sure you get a chance to speak to Nicholas about the Jews. When you do, speak freely—tell him everything—all about their persecutions. Try to convince him of the necessity for some humane treatment. It is you who must do this, Simanovitsch. It is you who must persuade him."

Before he left, Simanovitsch obtained the list of articles which the veterans wanted and the hospital couldn't supply. When he got home he telephoned Vyrubova, whose house rested within the palace grounds, to learn more about the morrow's celebration. Anna informed him that the Tsarevitch Alexis was to play the leading role in the services. He was going to present to the wounded men presents betokening the gratitude of Mama and Papa, and through them, the thanks of all of Russia. Simanovitsch then telephoned Alexis and inquired if the Tsarevitch wished him to bring anything with him when he came. The boy considered for a moment and then requested twelve silver watches, which he thought would make fine presents.

Simanovitsch labored through the night collecting the supplies that had been ordered and overseeing their arrangement in carts and wagons. Very early in the morning, not a bird's song after dawn, he set out with his caravan to Tsarskoye Selo. Before the Mass he had everything delivered and stowed away.

When Alexis saw the watches he smiled widely and said, "Ah, Simanovitsch, these are beautiful watches. The veterans will like them. Thank you."

Simanovitsch went to see to one last thing before the Mass started, and Alexis went straight to his mother to show her the sparkling gifts. But Alexandra was impressed more by the beaming face of her son than by the shining timepieces. Soon the time for the Mass was on hand, and the Imperial Family grouped themselves and paraded to the chapel.

During the ceremonies Rasputin walked over to the Tsar and said, "A son of the Jewish people stands before you, Nicholas."

Nicholas turned to face the peasant. "I don't know what you mean. What are you talking about?"

"Simanovitsch will explain it to you, Nicholas," said Rasputin. He motioned to his friend to advance. Simanovitsch approached the Tsar.

"Your Majesty," he began, "I have been living now for several years in your great capital city, and for me, personally, it has been a wonderful experience. But most of my people, scattered throughout the land, have not fared so well as I. They . . . "

Bishop Pitirim, standing within earshot on the other side of the Tsar, interrupted, "Simanovitsch, you claim to speak as a son of the Jewish people. Yet you speak indistinctly, there's a fog in your thoughts. Clear your brain and come to the point."

Simanovitsch cleared his throat and went back to the beginning.

"Your Majesty, what I have come to say to you is all very simple in the end. I shall try to be more explicit; please forgive me. What I want to say is this: My people suffer terribly at the hands of the Imperial laws. In Siberia and in the south they are murdered with impunity. They cry out for your support, Your Majesty. They say, 'Papa, Papa, if he only knew how we suffer, he would aid us.' "

As Simanovitsch watched Nicholas cooly listening to his speech, his heart sank and his legs seemed to turn into rubber. He saw his impassioned words pass the unperturbed face of the Tsar as so many annoyances to be brushed away and forgotten.

"Simanovitsch," Nicholas answered, "you have been a loyal friend of the Imperial Family for some years now. Through you, and our dear Father Grigori, Mama and I have been able to know very closely the conditions of our people. For you say, 'My people,' but they are also the Tsar's and the Tsarina's people. All the Russian people are our people. We must see to the welfare of all. We abhor the poverty and suffering of Russia's poor. But Simanovitsch, there are ninety million peasants and a hundred million foreign people on our Russian soil. These unfortunate ones suffer far more than your Jews. Why the Jews are wealthy compared to the peasants! When the peasants advance to the level of the Jews, then we shall talk about giving your people new laws."

Simanovitsch left his supplication to suffocate under these words. He knew further advocacy would merely be considered bad manners—and would gain nothing. He reported to the representatives of the Jews all over the land that he had brought their case to the Tsar and that Nicholas had turned it down.

When news of Nicholas' dismissal of the case made the rounds of the Jewish communities, a pervasive, lugubrious depression followed. People looked at one another out of great doleful black eyes, saying nothing, but renewing in the silence their ancient, tenacious compact to persist, whatever may come.

Never one to give in to resignation or self-pity, Simanovitsch reiterated his resolve to help his people. If the first major tactic failed, he joked, wasn't that what alternative plans were written for? To his friend Moses Ginsberg he said, "Well, then, and did you really expect Nicholas to come out four-square for the Jewish rights movement? Of course you didn't. No one did. We took a chance. It didn't pan out. So now we must begin again."

"Where do we go from here?" asked Ginsberg.

"Well, if we can't change the regime from the center outward, then we shall start somewhere off-center and work our way outward, inward, upward, downward, and around. Something's bound to give as we go. We shall settle for improvements. We shall concentrate our pressure on the ministry; we can use our money to good purpose there. You and I, Moses Ginsberg, shall bribe the Russian government into submission. Let's drink to our success." Thus the two millionaires forged their merry and not too impossible determination.

In his vigilance Simanovitsch received word that a certain Protopopov wished to become the Interior Minister; the office was vacant at that time. Simanovitsch quietly sought him out, introduced himself, and began a searching friendship with him. Protopopov soon learned to respect the extensive base of Simanovitsch's power, marveling that a Jew commanded so much respect from all levels of St. Petersburg society. As their friendship grew, the would-be minister, who came to know what simple things would please his newfound benefactor, showed himself willing to supply them, and his diligence repaid itself.

One evening at a gay, festive Christmas party at Princess Tarkanova's, Simanovitsch presented Protopopov to Rasputin. The peasant received this presentation civilly enough, but he was just too drunk and jovial to entertain many nonsensual thoughts that evening. The encounter served mostly to introduce Protopopov to the idiosyncrasies of Rasputin's behavior.

During the course of this interrogatory period, Simanovitsch drew

Protopopov out on his favorite topics. More than once he asked, "And what's your position on the war?"

"Simanovitsch," would come the answer, "why do you keep asking me the same questions over and over again? Do you think that my opinions change like the weather? You know, because I've told you five times already, what I feel about that disgusting war."

"Well said, my friend," returned Simanovitsch. "I repeat myself out of my concern for your cause. Don't take it to heart. I will not be the last one to ask you these questions."

And, indeed, the following weekend Protopopov found himself in a carriage with Vyrubova, Simanovitsch, and Rasputin escorting him to a rare dinner reception at the palace. Vyrubova entertained him throughout the trip with a barrage of her peculiarly intense questions. Simanovitsch just sat and smiled, enjoying the scenery and winking now and then to the beleaguered man.

Tsar Nicholas was at the front, but Alexandra hosted the small gathering in the graceful style of her smooth-mannered husband. Protopopov was more accustomed to this cooler, less harsh atmosphere, which reflected his ease and style admirably. The Tsarina noticed his savoir faire and was impressed by his easy comportment.

The next week Protopopov jumped over the final hurdle of his examination. Simanovitsch brought him before a group of the delegates of the Jews to answer their questions. Do you favor the Jewish rights movement? they asked him. What do you think about the residence requirements? And how do you feel about the traveling restrictions? Protopopov responded to all the questions to their satisfaction, and the following week he was finally appointed.

His accession to the delicate position was received with mixed emotions. The Jews were ebullient, of course, but the representatives to the Duma were indignant. They declaimed him as a puppet of the Imperial parties, and lashed out at him in their papers and pamphlets as a low form of plant life—a parasite, to be precise. But Rasputin set him straight concerning these gibing upholders of the people's honor. "They are dogs," he explained, "so use a leash, postpone the Duma; they won't bite."

Since Nicholas' departure for the front and the subsequent disintegration of Russian military organization, the members of the

Young Court had slipped ever downward into a sluggish depression, but the promises which the debonair, cool Protopopov held out for them acted as a kind of smelling salts that revived their spirit and activity.

One of the first orders he was called on to execute was the Tsar's decree deciding the fate of three Jewish sugar manufacturers, Hepner, Dobry, and Babushkin. The men had been accused of selling sugar to Germany and of delivering the merchandise to the enemy through Persia. The military authorities, who brought the charges against them, indicted them on three counts of state treason, conviction for each of which carried a mandatory death penalty.

The son of the chairman of the St. Petersburg synagogue, Seieuv, brought the story to Simanovitsch and offered to pay any amount necessary to bring justice to these men. After discussing the case with Rasputin, Simanovitsch agreed to sue for pardons. The first bill Seieuv received was for fifty thousand rubles to pay for a drinking banquet of Rasputin's.

Simanovitsch called Dobrovolsky, the Senate's Supreme State Attorney, onto the job. At a conference with him and the Justice Minister, the three decided their best tactic would be to attempt to get the case transferred to the civilian courts. The military authorities opposed this move, claiming that the case wasn't a civil concern, since the charges included speculation with the enemy—a crime whose chief victim was the army. General Batyushin's committee of investigation artfully presented its case.

Simanovitsch, seeking to inspire the off-hand Dobrovolsky to a more fiery concern, promised him the Justice Ministry if he succeeded in the case. He simultaneously sent his friend Jacob Rosen to each member of the General's committee, to glean all the information about the accusation he could, especially the weak parts of their argument. When this information came in a revived Dobrovolsky drew up a petition in the name of Hepner's daughter and presented it to the Empress.

There were no doubts about it: the men *had* sold a large quantity of sugar to Germany. The records revealed this in simple black and white figures. The shipment of the order through Persia was documented with similar clarity. But the loophole of the case—in this instance, a gaping aperture—was the similarly self-evident date of the deal—the summer of 1913, a full year before the hostilities had commenced!

Alexandra was duly impressed with the injustice of the military proceedings. She sent the petition to Nicholas at headquarters, where he also acknowledged the injustice and told General Batyushin that he planned to dismiss him as soon as he found a replacement. The General went to Simanovitsch pleading for his military skin. Simanovitsch offered to trade the General's integument for immediate transferral of the case to civilian courts, which was accomplished.

By this time Simanovitsch had secured for Dobrovolsky the post as Minister of Justice. In this position, Dobrovolsky called in the State's Attorney, reviewed the course of the investigations with him, and negotiated the suspension of the indictment.

But still the men weren't released. They had been awaiting the outcome of all this litigation down in the stockades of General Brusilov, commander of the Southwest Front. The General refused to acknowledge the authority of the Justice Ministry in what he saw as a clear-cut case of treason. So he sent the three to exile in Narim, a Northern Siberian territory.

Simanovitsch asked his friend, the attorney Sliosberg, to make up a second petition, this time acknowledging their guilt, but pleading for a pardon. He sent it to Nicholas, who in turn sent it to Protopopov for execution. The Interior Minister saw to it that all legal prosecution of the men ceased, and finally, just before the revolution, he obtained their release.

This case illustrates the need for patience and perseverance on the part of those who petitioned the throne. Another case, similar in its involutions and contortions, involved a vastly more spectacular figure—the greatest Jewish banker after the Rothschild family, Mr. Dimitri Rubinstein.

At the start of the war, Ivan Loginovitch Goremykin was Minister-President. His wife secured the job for him, and then insured it for him by treating Rasputin's palate daily to one of her dozen or so varieties of cooked potatoes. She brought them steaming hot to his house each evening, with a regularity which approached religious devotion. She felt her task was honorable and dignified, while Rasputin felt her potatoes were hearty and delicious. She also provided him with fish soup, white rolls, and apples, but she was known for her potatoes.

Rubinstein wished to meet Goremykin. A relationship with the Minister-President multiplied itself into contacts with many other people high up in the government and gave one chances to receive a great deal of governmental banking business. Besides, just the reputation alone of being Goremykin's friend tended to foster people's trust and confidence. So he asked Simanovitsch if there were any way he could arrange an interview.

Simanovitsch talked to Rasputin about it, and Rasputin, who knew and liked Rubinstein, agreed to talk to Goremykin. During their conversation, the Minister-President made some allusions to financial difficulties with his military hospital, and Rasputin took the hint. He reported to Simanovitsch that Rubinstein should make some contribution to the hospital. When Rubinstein heard this, he immediately went to the bank and took out a check for two hundred thousand rubles and brought it to Goremykin. From then on, the two met frequently.

One day, when Rasputin was at Tsarskoye Selo, Alexandra asked him if he knew of any bankers whom he trusted. He said that, as a matter of fact, he did—Dimitri Rubinstein. Rasputin filled her in with information about his background, friends, and extensive holdings. He told her about the old Jewish family that Rubinstein descended from and about his relative, Anton, the composer and pianist, and about some of Dimitri's financial coups.

Alexandra asked Rasputin to bring the banker to the palace some night, but to take care, for she wanted no one to see him coming into the palace, no one to see him while he attended on her, and no one to see him leaving. She wouldn't even tell Rasputin what she wanted a secret banker for, but neither was he dying to know.

Rasputin obeyed Alexandra's orders and duly presented Dimitri Rubinstein. The Empress' business was simple enough: she had some relatives in Germany who were in need and she had been accustomed to sending them an allowance out of her personal accounts. But since the start of hostilities with Germany she had been unable to send them the money. Now she wanted Rubinstein to arrange the sending of the money to them by some devious, secret route which could elude the watchful surveillance which constantly surrounded her. Of course, Rubinstein very willingly obliged the Empress, assuring her that he could send the money to them so secretly that even her relatives wouldn't know where it came from.

After this, Rasputin asked Rubinstein to come to his dinners many times. He sent many peasants to the banker, charging him with the responsibility of finding work for them. When Rubinstein ran out of positions to offer these men he created new offices, invented functions for them, and staffed them with Rasputin's petitioners. In this manner he and Rasputin forged a fast friendship. Banker Rubinstein became famous for his wealth and extensive connections not only in the Jewish community but in all of Russia.

Rubinstein owned one of the biggest insurance companies in the country, the Anchor Insurance Company. During the war he sold it to a Swedish firm. Since Anchor had insured many of the sugar factories in Ukrainia, he had to send the plans of the buildings of the factories to the Swedes. When Grand Duke Nicholas Nicholaievitch's men spied these prints in the mails destined for a foreign country they assumed they had stumbled on the greatest spy ring in all of Russia. Accordingly they arrested Rubinstein, thereby causing a sensation throughout Russia. The anti-Semites gloried in it; many Jewish people were taunted, spit upon, beaten, and even lynched.

In the meantime, Minister Goremykin had been replaced on the Ministry by Minister-President Sturmer; in short, Rubinstein's protection was gone. Alexandra, however, blanched when she heard the news that Rubinstein had been arrested for spying. If they discovered the connection she had had with him and—through him— with Germany, she would surely be charged with treason. The Empress called in the State's Attorney and commanded him to perform a secret investigation which would keep the lid on any data it gathered.

The Attorney went to headquarters and, together with a General Gurko, collected and organized all the evidence extant against the banker. They drew up a report concluding his innocence and sent it to Alexandra, who breathed a sigh of relief to see that the charges had not stemmed from Rubinstein's dealings with her. But General

Ruzsky got wind of the affair, transferred Rubinstein to Pleskau, and gave General Batyushin's commission the order to conduct a full military investigation of the charges.

Alexandra became furious when she heard this. "Is he trying to ruin me?" she cried. She went immediately to headquarters, obtained an order of release from Nicholas, sent it to Pleskau, and telegraphed Simanovitsch the news, so that he could pass it on to Mrs. Rubinstein. When she heard the news, Mrs. Rubinstein broke down in tears of joy and gratitude. She took the next train to Pleskau to meet her husband and take him home. But when she arrived at the palace at Pleskau, the commander, one of the Voyeikov brothers, refused to execute the Tsar's order. By some vagary, Rubinstein had been delivered into the hands of his worst, most passionate enemy.

A few years before, Dimitri Rubinstein had invited the Voyeikov brothers to enter with him into a partnership to found a bank in one of the Siberian territories. The bank had gone insolvent; Voyeikov had lost some eight hundred thousand rubles and was wiped out. Rubinstein had lost a similar amount, but he far more easily absorbed the loss. Now he was absorbing some of the animosity which his ill-fated suggestion had brought to pass. Moreover, Voyeikov was one of Nicholas' favorites.

Alexandra burnt with silent fury when she heard about Voyeikov's refusal. When her husband arrived home from the front, she went to him and brought him up on the disobedience of his friend, castigating him for allowing such behavior in a subordinate. Nicholas refused to rise to her challenge. He remained cool, taking in her wrath and calming it with his own indifference as he was used to do. When she had spent herself, he simply informed her that he had already passed down another order, this time directed to the warden of the prison, and that Rubinstein was probably already with his wife.

To carry this story through to the end, it is necessary to disrupt chronology and move ahead several months: when Nicholas had appointed Dobrovolsky Minister of Justice, Rasputin was already dead. Simanovitsch had been able to convince the Tsar that Dobrovolsky would have been Rasputin's choice. If the new stout Minister of Justice was a limited man, nevertheless he had helped

Simanovitsch to obtain the pardon of the three Kiev sugar manufacturers and had helped him get a lot of work done in the senate. So Simanovitsch had preferred his name to Tsar Nicholas.

The Minister belonged to the Old Court, however. He had long ago sold his soul to their cause for a considerable amount of support and money. Simanovitsch knew that Dobrovolsky wasn't above taking a bribe, but he didn't in the least suspect that he had seated a member of the Old Court.

After the scene related above, the Minister of Justice went to the Tsar and argued with him against Rubinstein's release. He charged the banker with espionage and made such a telling case against him that Nicholas acceded to his advice and canceled the order which was to have removed the indictment.

When Simanovitsch learned from Mrs. Rubinstein that her husband had been arrested a second time, he was furious. It didn't take him long to find out what had happened, and as soon as he did he marched straight over to Dobrovolsky's home.

"How could you do such a thing?" Simanovitsch said. "After all Rubinstein and I have done for you. What kind of an ungrateful ball of flesh are you, anyway?"

"But Simanovitsch," said Dobrovolsky, "I didn't go to Nicholas and incite him to do it. We were talking about something entirely removed from the case. He brought it up himself. He simply informed me that he had changed his mind, that he had reconsidered the evidence. I merely gave my opinion of the wisdom of his conclusion. That's all."

"Dobrovolsky, you are a lying reprobate, and I shall have nothing more to say to you. Not now or ever. Consider yourself finished, for I shall not rest until Nicholas sees your perniciousness." And Simanovitsch stormed out of the house.

The next day Simanovitsch went to see Alexandra. When he had told her what had happened at Dobrovolsky's the night before, she turned on him and exclaimed, "Simanovitsch, what have you done? Do you want to destroy us all? How could you speak to the Minister of Justice like that? Why did you have to make such an enemy of him?"

"But, Your Majesty," insisted Simanovitsch, exasperated, "I did not *make* an enemy of him last night. He has always *been* our enemy. I merely exposed the fact. Do you think it would be any safer for any of us if I let him tiptoe around under cover of his lies?"

"I don't know. But what's to happen to us now? We're all ruined." And the Empress' cheeks were wetted with hot tears of despair.

"Alexandra," Simanovitsch more calmly intoned, "we must be strong, especially now. We must fight back. We must get Dobrovolsky out of power. What do you think we should do? How should we get him put out of our way?"

"Simanovitsch, I don't know," the Empress answered. "Go to Protopopov. He will have some plan. Yes. He will save us. Go to the Interior Minister and tell him I told you he must do something about this mess. He must clean it up. Go and tell him."

Protopopov was shocked by the news. He, too, was surprised by Dobrovolsky's betrayal. "Our friend thinks he has Nicholas' undying favor," Protopopov said, attempting to analyze the situation. "He thinks that Nicholas believes that he was Rasputin's choice. That makes him brave."

"Nicholas does believe he was Rasputin's choice," returned Simanovitsch, dolefully. "I told him so myself when I argued with him to appoint him. Good God, what have I done?"

"Now, Simanovitsch, don't you go to pieces too," snapped the Minister. "I'll call him up now."

Protopopov rang up Dobrovolsky and reprimanded him sharply for his actions. But Dobrovolsky stuck to his story that he had had nothing to do with the Tsar's decision. When Protopopov reported this to his friend, Simanovitsch almost spat.

"Okay, then," he said, "we shall just have to do it the hard way, Scriblkantz. Thanks anyway for your help."

"What's the hard way?" asked Protopopov.

"We shall have to buy Dimitri's release."

"Well, that shouldn't be too hard—Rubinstein's a wealthy man, isn't he?" queried Protopopov.

"Yes, that he is, for sure. But it means that whenever I want anything out of that worm in the future I shall have to offer him something. That is the hard part."

Simanovitsch went to see the grieving wife and took her to the

bank where she withdrew one hundred thousand rubles. Simanovitsch brought a box of jewels along, for he knew that Dobrovolsky's daughter had just announced her engagement and that the
gemstones would make a fine dowry. He was counting on Dobrovolsky's inability to forfeit such goods in the cause of honesty.

The short meeting took place in his offices. Mrs. Rubinstein was
very simple and direct.

"Here is a hundred thousand rubles, Justice Minister," she said as
she handed him the thick envelope. "I want you to release my
husband."

The Justice Minister wasn't surprised. "But of course, Mrs.
Rubinstein. And how are you today, Simanovitsch?" he asked as he
began thumbing the bills to ascertain that the right amount was
there.

"Don't you joke with me, Justice Minister," Simanovitsch shot
back. "Take these gems. I know of Sonia's engagement; see that
they get to *her*."

The meeting ended as soon as the Minister counted the bills and
assured the two that he would secure the release of the banker that
week.

But Rubinstein didn't gain his freedom that week, nor any week
soon after. The Justice Minister's conscience spoke a peculiar
language. He went back on his promise to secure the release, but he
did remove the banker from the fetid conditions of Russian penal
life and had him transferred to a pleasant sanitarium in the Caucasus
mountains. Here he could receive visitors, presents, and the prefer-
ential treatment he had been accustomed to.

The revolution interrupted all of Simanovitsch's attempts to
extracate his friend from the legal thickets. During Kerensky's
government, Mrs. Rubinstein availed herself of a good lawyer and
brought the case to this more moderate man. Rubinstein was finally
freed in the spring of 1917.

ELEVEN

One morning before dawn the Empress' personal courier summoned Simanovitsch. He quickly dressed, forewent his breakfast appointment with Rasputin, and entered his carriage for a half-awake ride to the palace.

They met in the Tsarina's boudoir. For once, perhaps under the influence of the hour, Alexandra came right to the point: "Simanovitsch," she said, "I want you to disassemble the tiara."

"But Empress," replied Simanovitsch, "what can this mean? This isn't mere jewelry which can be fashioned to the will. The tiara is State property. It belongs to no single individual. I couldn't think of dismantling it. It would be treason!"

"Oh, Simanovitsch," Alexandra said, "don't you think I know the tiara is the property of the State?"

"Then why do you wish me to take it apart?" asked Simanovitsch.

"Because I am afraid."

"Of whom, Your Majesty?"

"I don't know," said the Empress, looking fretfully about. "Everyone, I suppose. They are all against us, you know, Simanovitsch. They are all just lying out there in wait for us to make the right mistake. Poor Nicholas. Things have gone so badly."

"But, Empress, do you propose that I commit State treason because of your fears? Surely, what can this accomplish? Who benefits by such folly?"

These were strong words to use in conversation with the Empress of Russia, but Simanovitsch was always cranky in the morning, and this woman's petulant command riled his sense of propriety. Alexandra was not to be dissuaded. She moved over to a mahogony chest, produced a small key from a bracelet on her wrist, and opening the chest, lifted out the felt-covered crown and carried it back to her seat and unshrouded it.

Simanovitsch was stunned. He had never seen the piece at such proximity before. The dawn light reflected off the diamonds and pearls, the gold and rubies, dazzling and wonderful. Never had a work of man sent such shivers up his spine.

"Simanovitsch, I don't want to lose this," she said, and then added, "Have you ever seen a more magnificent piece? Even Fabergé could not dream it."

He took the tiara in his hands and held it up to the morning light. Few jewelers had ever beheld such a monument to their trade. He fished out his monocle from his pocket.

"Magnificent!" he murmured. "Truly magnificent. Alexandra, how could you ask me to disassemble such a triumph? Truly, I do not understand."

"Simanovitsch, I want you to bring it out of the country. I don't want to see anything happen to it. You must take it apart and smuggle it out of the country. Send it to America. Some day we shall assemble it again. But now we must hide it."

Simanovitsch smiled broadly, almost intoxicated with the beams and the glow of the object.

"Alexandra," he said, "I shall do as you ask." And he padded out of the palace with a sure grasp on the cold dull weight of the gold and diamond tiara.

He went straight back to his house and had a light breakfast, then telephoned Rasputin to tell him that he would stop in later, after dinner.

All morning and all afternoon Simanovitsch worked on the tiara with a special set of tools which he normally kept in a small unknown workroom at the back of the third story of his house. He extracted each jewel with minute care and plopped it into its own little black velvet pouch. These little bags he gathered into an oaken box with a special lock in his safe. There was no sense in shipping the gold settings to America; why incur the risk and the cost when it could easily be reproduced over there? The gold could be melted down after casts were made. This he would have to have done in his shop, where he had the smelting ovens.

Later that evening Simanovitsch called for his carriage to be brought around and set off for 64 Gorokhovaya to dine with Rasputin. It was a dusky, bitter cold evening. Simanovitsch had been hard at work all day, and his weary bones rebelled against the weather's insult.

Rasputin saw the faint blueness in his friend's face and hustled him swiftly into the study where a ruddy fire proffered a warm welcome. The port was ready to soothe Simanovitsch's innards, and in a matter of minutes he relaxed and felt all the day's tension melt in the fiery glow of Rasputin's hospitality.

The peasant's day had been equally tiresome. He had spent it at the Theological Academy, among the bishops and priests of the highest echelons of the Church. There had been a reception for one newly mitered, but it was a stuffy affair. Rasputin had no stomach for civic conventions such as this and looked forward to an evening's vinous frolic. Already two empty port bottles littered the hearth rug. There would be more before dawn.

"You're looking a little peaked, Aaron," said Rasputin. "You shouldn't work so hard; it puts a cramp in the soul."

Simanovitsch looked archly across at his friend. "The idea is to achieve a balanced existence: work over play equals one, unity. The ratio of the cosmos."

"Oh, but you are too practical. What is life, if it isn't pleasure? Eh? You can work all day polishing your little baubles. What good are those silly stones if they put a pain in your bones, eh? To light up the bosoms of Russia's fairest, is that your cosmic ratio? My God, man, you have to take them off there before the fairest can really shine anyway! And those damned latches—it is a conspiracy you jewelers make to thwart the passions of real men. Passion, Simanovitsch, that's my ratio: man on woman makes one; *that* is the cosmic unity. *That's* where life happens."

And to underscore his point, Rasputin chucked the third empty bottle into the fireplace, and opened another one.

"Do you mean to tell me that that's the posture of real men?"

Simanovitsch chided. "Come on, my friend. Could the God above have created any more ludicrous position for us to carry on His work? Surely you don't mean to tell me that we are ourselves only in that ridiculous posture! Surely the world was conceived out of a more dignified stance."

"But is it not written, my friend," returned the peasant, " 'Be fruitful and multiply and replenish the earth'? And so I am right; it is our call from God."

"Ah, but your quotation doesn't go far enough," cried Simanovitsch in glee. "Is it not further written: ' . . . and subdue the earth; and have dominion over the fish of the sea, and over the fowl of the air, and over every living thing that moveth upon the earth'? Now *that* is the whole story. We are lords of creation, Rasputin; you would have us wallow in the mud like mere animals. You would deny us our lordship, Rasputin." Simanovitsch stared fiercely into the flames and opened his own bottle.

"Humph," grunted the peasant, and he finished the fourth bottle and tossed it to the ground with a thud. "So we are, Simanovitsch. So we are. Nevertheless, as we may be lords with the whip and slaughter-knife, so we are gods with our bodies. *This* is the instrument of creation," he shouted, thumping his chest loudly with his palm. "This, my friend, is the pinnacle of our achievement," he cried, clutching his groin. "No bridge was built, no city constructed that ever danced, or made itself over again. No, my friend, I remain unconvinced of your equation, but we shall not argue any more now. Let us go to the kitchen and eat."

In the first throes of drunkenness and hunger, both men walked rather tipsily through the dark rooms. In the kitchen, attended by Rasputin's nieces, they ate fish soup, potatoes, black bread, and cheese. Talk was sparse. When he had swallowed his final mouthful, Rasputin burped deeply and poured out the remains of the sixth bottle. Simanovitsch followed shortly after, wiping his mouth on the coarse napkin.

"Shall we leave these two fine ladies to their work?" said Rasputin.

"Ay," said Simanovitsch, "we had best attend our fire or it'll be out before we know it."

They moved back to the study where they found, to their great dismay, gray ashes devoid of embers. Aaron went back to the kitchen for kindling and embers, while Rasputin went out back for logs. In twenty minutes they were seated once again before an orange blaze. Suddenly Maria burst into the room.

"Father," she panted, "the Empress is on the phone. She's in an awful state. Come quickly."

Rasputin gave Simanovitsch a knowing look and trotted out of the room to pick up the line in the kitchen.

"Hello, Your Majesty," he began. "What has happened?"

"Oh, Father Grigori," the Empress cried, "poor Alexis, my poor darling boy. He's fallen off a chair and bruised his knee. His leg is like a balloon and he's screaming so pitifully. Oh Father Grigori, you must do something, you must!" The Empress dissolved into a flurry of tears.

Rasputin waited patiently at his end of the line for the Empress' outburst to subside into sniffles. Then he said, "Alexandra, you must have faith during crises. God knows of your boy's affliction and hears his childish pleas. Do not feel so foresaken. Pray to God in your heart, and now bring the phone to Alexis, for I wish to speak to him also."

The heartbroken mother took comfort in the soothing tones of Rasputin's voice. Softly she went back into Alexis' bedroom and sat on the edge of the boy's bed. She picked up the extension, saying, "My darling, Father Grigori wants to talk to you."

The boy took hold of the receiver with a whitened little hand.

"Father Grigori?" he sobbed.

"Alexis, my boy, I hear you fell off a chair. Heh?"

"Oh, yes, Father, on my knee, and it hurts so bad . . . ," and the Tsarevitch began to whimper once again.

"Now, Alexis, listen to me. I can't hear you listening. Let me hear you listen, and I will help you. Do you want Father Grigori to help you? Do you?"

"Oh, yes," he sniffed.

"Well, then, you must let me hear you listening to me. Go on. You must put the receiver closer to your ear. That's it. I can almost hear you," he purred. "That's a good boy."

The boy concentrated on letting Rasputin hear his ear listen, and the monk kept up a steady stream of low, purling chatter. But soon the boy's tight grip relaxed as he felt a new consciousness emerge into his mind, a hope, a trust, a real vibrant emotion spawned by the monk's gentle yet powerful presence. And gradually this new feeling absorbed the shrill pain in his limb, and the Tsarevitch gave himself up entirely to the reassuring voice. In a quarter of an hour he had slipped into a restful sleep. The progress of his hemorrhage halted, and finally the blood ebbed.

When he returned to his study, Rasputin found Simanovitsch pondering the flames.

"Oh, it's all right now. I put him to sleep. He'll be better in the morning."

"What happened?"

"He fell off a chair. I can't tell who suffers most, Alexis or Alexandra."

"Rasputin," asked Simanovitsch, "why do you let them go on like that?"

"What do you mean?" snapped Rasputin, offended.

"Well . . ."

"Say what you mean, Jew," said Rasputin with menace in his eyes.

"Why don't you make an end of this business of Alexis? Why put him to sleep when you can bring him back to health? Aren't you trifling with the boy?"

Rasputin sat back in his leather chair and opened another bottle. He said nothing immediately, but sat staring over at his friend as if he were a creature of another species, far remote from his own world. He drank his dark wine in great gurgling swallows.

"Simanovitsch," he said finally, "what would happen if Alexis became whole?"

"I don't know," said Simanovitsch. "I suppose those at Tsarskoye Selo would begin to live decent lives."

"And what of me? What kind of a life would I then lead?"

"I don't know."

"You don't know," mimicked the peasant. "The *hell* you don't know," he bellowed. "I'd be back at Pokrovskoye, flirting with village girls. And where would you be, my fine friend? Eh? You'd be back in Kiev making wedding bands for peasants!"

"I do not understand you in the least," protested Simanovitsch. "If it is wealth and position you want, why do you live here in this boardinghouse? Why, you could be sheltered in a palace, clothed in silk, and attended by a host!"

"You are vain like the rest," sighed Rasputin, "content with cloth and jewels. They are dead objects, but this house suits me fine. My clothes keep me warm in the winter and cool in the summer. My larder is never bare, and my bed is sturdy—my life is full. And I dare you to deny it."

"But if you had gold you could live the same full life, only better," Simanovitsch answered. "You would not need a poor little boy's suffering to assure you your place."

"Simanovitsch," replied Rasputin, "you seem to think that I choose to leave the boy in his pain to gain a high position near the throne. You say I trifle with the boy's life, and then you turn around and say that I do not demand enough compensation for these services."

"What I mean, Novitch, is this: You should get enough gold to support you and then cure Alexis once and for all. Make a clean thing of it."

"My friend, a man like me is born infrequently in time. I can do many wonderful things, but I cannot do all the things one might want me to do. I am ashamed of you, for believing me so callous as to serve my own interest with a little boy's agony. I do not know why God has afflicted Alexis with such a horrible disease, but he has, and I cannot change God's will!"

Simanovitsch took this admission in silence, not wanting to decide right then whether he believed his friend. A long pause developed. But each man was a veteran in the arts of friendship, and soon their spirits rose from out of this sore interlude. As dawn filtered through the curtained windows, the assortment of dead wine bottles had grown into a mound.

TWELVE

Through the summer and fall of 1916, Russia's military organization slipped rapidly toward disintegration under the advance of the German machine. As the Russian battle casualties reached into the millions, Nicholas' determination to fight on to a military victory lapsed. Sensing this, Rasputin pressed forward his propaganda against the war. The newspaper which Rasputin had Witte and Simanovitsch's friends purchase increased the outcry against the hostilities. Nicholas started looking for ways out.

The problem was that Russia had allied herself to France by the treaty of 1912. By the terms of the treaty, she couldn't negotiate a separate peace with Germany. Both France and England made great efforts to encourage the continuation of the Russian war effort. Rasputin, internationally known as an advocate of peace, was vilified by the British press. The French Ambassador, Maurice Paléologue, arranged an interview with the peasant in hopes of persuading him over to the Gallic logic. Rasputin merely insulted him. The English Ambassador, more shrewd than his Parisien confrère, sent a well-made young Englishwoman to paint Rasputin's portrait. Her mission was to win the peasant's heart and change his mind. After six months, however, Rasputin kicked her out of his house.

One day in the early autumn Rasputin convoked an informal meeting of special individuals. He had invited Vladimir Khabalov, the Commander of the St. Petersburg Garrison; General Boris Globachev, Chief of the Political Police; Leo Nikitin, Commander of the St. Petersburg Fortress; and Interior Minister Protopopov. The latter used his discretion to bring General Kurlov.

Rasputin opened the meeting with a question. "The discussion we are about to engage in carries a heavy burden of responsibility. Can everyone here be trusted to uphold that burden? Does anyone here dispute the trustworthiness of any of our members?"

No one said anything, so Protopopov answered, "Rasputin, I suppose we all share a mutual trust. Why have you brought us together?"

"I am sorry to hear you say that, Minister," Rasputin returned, "for I don't trust everyone here. If I had known you would have made the unfortunate alliance with General Kurlov that you apparently have, then I would never have allowed you into the Ministry in the first place."

General Kurlov smiled sardonically at the peasant, nodded a good-bye to the others, and left the room.

"Now then, my friends," Rasputin began, "I have arranged this little meeting today to speak to you about the Tsar's plans for conducting peace. He can't make a treaty while he is bound to France. To relieve this situation he has commissioned me to engineer a mock insurrection in the capital. When these demonstrations occur, he can then say to France that the throne will fall unless he makes peace—and voilà, we make a pact with Germany. I have talked to Doctor Dubrovin, of the horrible Union of the Russian People, who has the job of bringing the insurgents up from the Caucasus. You, Khabalov, and Nikitin will take charge of dispersing these people. But you must take care not to act too swiftly. We want a general demonstration of the people, not a tiny riot. Don't act too soon. And you must use only young men, not old ones who will act with too much competence. It must look real. But use experienced officers. We cannot risk too much. And the men must be loyal to the Tsar. Or else it will be real. So take care."

The details of the plan were hashed out, and the artificial uprising was planned for the end of October.

During the last five years of his career, Rasputin's enemies had grown in number daily. The possibility that they would send an assassin after him prompted the establishment of an intertwining security web of political police, Simanovitsch's agents, and friendly military figures. General Globachev's force surveyed Rasputin's home night and day and reported regularly to the General. A second set of agents followed the peasant wherever he went. Increasingly, Simanovitsch tried to keep in close touch with his friend, stopping at his house each morning for breakfast and communicating by telephone when business forced his absence.

In spite of these precautions, a number of assassins leveled their hatred at Rasputin's unkempt head. The first one to draw blood was sent on her mission by Rasputin's old enemy, the monk Iliodor. Before he had been forced to leave Russia, Iliodor had exercised a soul-renewing moral influence on a certain veteran prostitute named Guseva. She was a Russian peasant woman, with the same roots and temperament as Rasputin himself. In the heat of her conversion, Iliodor had ripped open her blouse and placed around her neck a chain which suspended a knife over her panting bosom. "Take this holy instrument of the Lord," he exhorted, "and bring God's justice to the anti-Christ."

Guseva traveled to Pokrovskoye, and all during the spring established herself as a hard-working, pious member of the village. When Rasputin, home for his annual summer visit, was on his way out of his house one morning, she flew up to him and cried, "Give alms to the poor in the name of God." As the peasant fumbled with his purse, the broken-nosed, steel-faithed peasantwoman ripped the knife off her neck and plunged it into Rasputin's abdomen.

His intestines herniating through his belly, he hobbled back to his house. Guseva screamed, "You shall die, you black-souled devil! The Lord punishes!" And she lunged to finish the Lord's vengeance. But Rasputin parried her thrust with a small log he was able to pick up as he reached the porch of his cottage. Hearing the shouts of the crazed woman, a number of people quickly converged on the scene. Rasputin was helped indoors. The crowd quickly grew ugly, thrashed Guseva, and prepared to lynch her on the spot. Rasputin, however, sent out word to let her go.

The doctor of the village did his best to attend to the wound, but Rasputin disdained his art. He allowed him only to wash off the blood. When that was done he sent for his herb pouch, poked around in it until he found the necessary plants, and then applied them to the gash, making his own bandage. In six weeks the peasant looked fit as a fiddle, defying all the morbid predictions of the Tsar's medical attendants.

The conspiracy had nearly succeeded; only Rasputin's supernatural vitality and knowledge of folk medicine had preserved him from death. If he had known the end in store for him—the brutal coldness of the massive conspiracy which finally did succeed—perhaps Rasputin would have preferred to have his life cut short by this kindred, passionate sinner. But his powers of prophecy, as is so often the case, did not give him a window on his own future, except on one significant occasion which will be documented later. His confidence increased, and so did his enemies.

In 1916, at the peak of Rasputin's power, they struck.

Simanovitsch caught the first hints of the conspiracy from a former employee, Alexei Magorsky, who had worked for him in the Fireman Club. Tomilen, the Supreme Mayor of Pleskau, had been on the Fireman Club's Board of Directors. Then the National Club, an association of reactionary elements, elected Tomilen as their president. Knowing the good work of the young Alexei and his friend Ivan, Tomilen asked Simanovitsch if he could bring the two to his new club. Simanovitsch acceded to this request, glad to be able to infiltrate the National Club with his own agents.

Alexei came to him one day to tell him of a council which had just broken up at the National Club. His friend Ivan had served the men. Sensing something amiss from the fragments of conversation which he had been able to catch, he unburdened himself to his friend after the affair. Given the nature of the information, Alexei then considered it prudent to inform Simanovitsch.

Repeatedly, the group had mentioned the Tsar, the Tsarina, and Rasputin. The chairman of the meeting, a delegate to the Duma, Vladimir Purishkevitch, had mentioned Rasputin's name with a peculiar disgust. But his tone was tinged with that quality of elated finality to be found in the voice of any man planning the relief of an intolerable burden. Other members of the group which Ivan had been able to recognize were the Grand Duke Dimitri Pavlovitch,

Count Tatishchev, Prince Felix Yusupov, and the ex-Interior Minister Khvostov.

Simanovitsch took this news in with the greatest concern. He sent Alexei back to the club with a thousand rubles to split with Ivan and orders to continue the surveillance of the premises. Simanovitsch had a friend, a certain Doctor Salvasan, who ran a clinic on the Nevsky Prospect which specialized in the treatment of various venereal diseases. He knew, too, that Vladimir Purishkevitch was afflicted with one of these diseases, and that, in fact, this doctor was treating him for it. So Simanovitsch visited his medical friend and prevailed upon him to lift the dictates of his professional integrity long enough to aid in the preserving of the life of the Imperial couple and Rasputin. For a sufficient amount, Doctor Salvasan agreed to question Purishkevitch about the conspiracy against the peasant.

Poised over the Duma delegate's derrière, his hands engaged in injecting some drug into him, the doctor asked Purishkevitch what he thought about "that peasant, Rasputin." Purishkevitch was silent a moment and declared that Russia would be rid of that vile blight within the next three days, and that all of the Duma, including the president, Rodzianko, agreed with him.

When this was relayed to Simanovitsch, he went immediately to Tsarskoye Selo to inform the Tsarina through the Vaskoboynikov sisters. Then he went back to Rasputin's and was brutally frank.

"You must go to Nicholas at headquarters," he told him. "You must warn him of the urgency of the situation. You must tell him that a *coup d'état* is imminent. Nicholas must renounce you. You must make him publicly disclaim you. Ask him for a million pounds sterling and flee to Palestine. You will be killed if you stay here another day."

Rasputin listened to all this in a silent, moody perplexity. He called for his wine, drank two quick glasses, and stood up before the fireplace, staring into the flames.

"No," he finally said to Simanovitsch. "I shall not go to Nicholas. It is premature. The nobles are against me. They know I shall end this filthy war. They hate me. They are not true Russians. They have no true Russian blood. They are against me because I am for the peasants, the true Russians. I shall make peace first, then I shall leave. We shall go through with the plan."

At that moment, Pakarchadkadze, the fiancé of one of Rasputin's daughters, entered the dining room and invited Rasputin to come with him to a banquet at Count Tolstoi's. Prince Eristov's carriage waited outside to carry them there.

Relieved to find an escape from the deadening weight of Siman-ovitsch's anxiety, Rasputin readily assented to the apparently spontaneous invitation. The Prince's carriage took them to the Count's house on Tretskaya Street. The party raged through several of the Count's huge salons and boasted a large collection of the Imperial society's most luminous personages. Rasputin felt completely at ease, quickly picking up the pace of the party. By eleven o'clock he had imbibed enough wine to drown a normal man.

He was standing in the central salon, next to the bar, just in the process of uncorking his ninth bottle of wine, when he saw, as if through a mist, Pakarchadkadze across the room drawing his revolver and leveling it at him. All of a sudden Rasputin crashed the bottle against the nearby stone fireplace and yelled, pointing at Pakarchadkadze: "You want to kill me, but your hand doesn't obey!"

The man froze under the paralyzing effects of Rasputin's glare. The whole party ground to a halt in a matter of a few seconds. The young man stood there in the center of the room with his arm extended into the silence. Rasputin stood facing him across the room, panting in his emotion. He eyes leveled an intense gaze across the room to the would-be assassin. Rasputin's vibrating, preter-natural authority disintegrated the youngster's will. He could find no solution to his shameful position, so he turned the gun on himself and sent a bullet into his chest. Other partygoers rushed to his aid.

Later, when Simanovitsch heard that an "incident" had occurred at the Count's during the party, he asked Rasputin what had happened. The peasant was elated. The attack had come, he explained to Simanovitsch, but he had been too strong for them. His power had conquered. He was now out of danger.

Simanovitsch was not reassured, however; he refused to believe that the conspiracy had arranged only this paltry attempt and would cease with this one defeat. He told Rasputin what he felt, but the peasant would hear no more of the voice of reason. He had exerted himself last night in a ferocious test of his energies and he considered the plot to be up. Simanovitsch, finding he could do nothing with Rasputin this morning, decided to confer with General Globachev and check back later.

When he returned in the afternoon he learned from the police agents watching the house that Grand Duke Dimitri Pavlovitch had driven up to the house, stayed for about twenty minutes, and departed alone. Simanovitsch questioned Rasputin. Yes, the Grand Duke had visited him and had invited him to come to tea. Hearing this, Simanovitsch knew the conspiracy was at last in the open.

"If you go to the Grand Duke's for tea," he said, "you are a vain fool and deserve the fate they have in store for you there."

"Your concern is idiotic," mocked Rasputin. "They are a bunch of schoolboys. They wouldn't dare try anything. They have seen my power. I can conquer them at will."

"I forbid you to go," steamed Simanovitsch.

"You, or anyone else, can forbid me to do *nothing*," shouted Rasputin. "The devil take you all. I'm tired of all this whining and quaking in the face of a few pimps. They have already made their moves. They won't try again. Besides, if they do, I shall vanquish them as I have done in the past. Go. Leave me to myself. Today I shall drink twenty bottles of wine, take my bath, and go to sleep. God will speak to me during the night. Tomorrow I shall know that my power has conquered."

Simanovitsch took satisfaction in this schedule. At least Rasputin would be safe until the morning. He left, after checking with the agents, and went home to a restless night.

In the morning he arrived to find that Alexandra and one of her daughters had stopped in earlier at Rasputin's in the guises of two Red Cross sisters to warn him of the conspiracy and to exhort him to take care. Bishop Isidor also stopped by that morning to let them know that he, too, had heard of the plot and that, as far as he was concerned, Rasputin ought to lay low for the next few days. The Court lady, Lydia Nikitina, also stopped by with words of caution.

Simanovitsch grew steadily more concerned as these messengers added their warnings to his. He spoke to Rasputin in the late afternoon.

"What are you going to do, Rasputin?" he asked.

"I don't know. I shall wait for the Little One to call. Then I shall go," he answered.

"Who is this person you call the Little One? I have never heard you speak of him before," asked Simanovitsch.

"I shall not tell you, so don't ask," snapped Rasputin, who was growing weary of all this unwanted solicitude.

Simanovitsch was terrified; he was sure that the strange new words had something to do with the plot. But when Rasputin once made up his mind, it was impossible to try and get him to change it. Simanovitsch went to Protopopov for reinforcement.

Protopopov came back with Simanovitsch to Rasputin's, and together they checked the security forces. Nothing was amiss; no one had come, Rasputin hadn't left. The two men went inside to while away the afternoon. At dinner time Rasputin appeared looking very sulky. Protopopov extracted a promise from him that he would not leave the house that evening.

Night fell, cold and dark. Rasputin retired early. As an extra precaution, Simanovitsch locked away his fur coat in the wardrobe. Seeing how bone-weary the Jew looked, Protopopov sent him home to get some rest, waited until Rasputin fell asleep, and then went out to check the guard. Leaving them with orders to subdue Rasputin if he attempted to go out of the house, Protopopov went home confident.

Near midnight on December 29, 1916, Rasputin received a visitor. He went outside, informed the guard that he was going to spend the night at home, distributed some money, and exhorted the freezing men to seek food and warmth at an inn. He called Simanovitsch, told him that the Little One had come, that he was going out with him, and that he would call back at two o'clock.

Simanovitsch pleaded with Rasputin to remain at home, repeating his conviction that they would kill him if he went out. But Rasputin was obdurate.

Simanovitsch knew that sleep would be impossible. He woke up his son Semion, and they sat before the phone, waiting. One-thirty came; two; two-thirty. Finally, three o'clock struck and Rasputin hadn't called.

"Listen to me, Semion," said Simanovitsch, "Rasputin is dead. God help us all now."

"What shall we do, father?" asked Semion.

"We must wake Maria and Varia, and tell them what has happened. Perhaps they can tell us who this Little One is."

Simanovitsch and his son went to Rasputin's, woke up the daughters and told them, as best as they could, what they were convinced had happened.

"Have you ever heard of this Little One?" asked Simanovitsch.

"No, Simanovitsch, we've never heard of him," said Varia.

"No, never," repeated Maria.

"Is it that you never heard of him or that Rasputin has asked you to keep his name a secret? Heh? Which one is it? Tell me," demanded Simanovitsch, getting more and more excited.

"Rasputin has told us never to tell anyone, especially you, Simanovitsch. He made us promise," said Maria.

"But I tell you that the Little One may have killed your father! Don't you understand? He may have been a trap. We must find him now, before it's too late. It may be too late already. Who is this man? You've got to tell me."

"Felix Yusupov," said Varia. "But don't tell father that we told you."

"But Yusupov was his enemy. How did he ever get Rasputin's confidence?"

"Munia Golovina brought them together," said Maria. "She knows where they were going. Ask her."

Simanovitsch and his son flew over to the home of Munia Golovina. It was by this time about four o'clock. They awakened the young woman and Simanovitsch said, "Munia Golovina, Rasputin has been killed. We must find his body. Where did he go tonight?"

"No, Simanovitsch, you are wrong. Rasputin isn't dead. Why, I just saw him a few hours ago with Prince Yusupov."

"Munia, they have killed him. It was a conspiracy. How did the Prince win back the trust of Rasputin? What has happened?" asked Simanovitsch.

"You know, Simanovitsch," began the sleepy woman, "that Felix wasn't—well, quite normal, sexually. He liked men. So his parents sent him to Rasputin so that Rasputin would hypnotize him and change him. Then later, when Felix wanted to marry Irina—you know she's the daughter of the Grand Duke Alexander Mikhailovitch and the Grand Duchess Xenia Alexandrovna, the Tsar's sister—well, Rasputin would hear nothing of it. He didn't like Felix. I guess he didn't really cure him. Anyway, they aren't of Russian blood, those Yusupovs—Tartars, really. And that was another point against the marriage in Rasputin's eyes. But the Grand Duke wanted to have Felix as a son-in-law. I suppose for his estates. So the marriage came off.

"Well, Felix has just been promoted to officer from the military academy. He wants to be in the palace guard. Who doesn't want to be in Nicholas' guard? I tell you, Simanovitsch, those parties are something! Anyway, Nicholas won't permit any of his kind into his flock. It causes problems, you know. So Felix asked me to bring him to Rasputin so that he could ask him to help him with Nicholas. They met tonight. Now they are gone to a celebration party at the Prince's. The Princess is there. Rasputin wanted to meet her and Felix wanted to show her off. So that's where they are right now, Simanovitsch. It's a perfectly normal banquet. I'm sure Rasputin is with the Princess right now."

"I'm afraid," said Simanovitsch, "that both you and Rasputin have been tricked. Princess Yusupova has been in the Crimea all month visiting her relatives. She's not due back here until Christmas. Thank you, Munia Golovina. You should go back to sleep now. Tomorrow you will need all your strength. We shall all need our strength."

Simanovitsch and his son excused themselves and left the house. It was then about four-thirty in the morning.

About four hours earlier, a little after midnight, a car had driven up to the younger Prince Yusupov's palace. The servant came out to open the doors and was dismissed for the rest of the night. Four men got out of the car—Dimitri Pavlovitch, Purishkevitch, and Felix Yusupov, and Rasputin. It was a beastly cold night and the men hurried indoors.

As they entered the hallway of the palace, they were greeted by the butler who started to handle their overcoats. The Prince dismissed him for the night. They entered the salon to their right and walked in. There were two women in the large room. One was seated on a white silk divan at the far end of the room, the other stood with a teacup in her hands, apparently in a state of nervous agitation.

A young man stepped out from behind some curtains which draped a French window and shot Rasputin in the eye. The three other men drew pistols and put a total of ten more bullets into his collapsed body. One of the women screamed.

The young man who had fired first went over to the bloody body, kicked it, and then said, "Where shall we put him, Felix?"

"I don't know," he said.

"But Felix, we must do something with him. We can't leave him in your front rooms, now, can we? Here, help me drag him to the basement."

The men carried the limp form down into the dank basement of the old building. They laid it on a pile of coal and went upstairs. The hour was one o'clock.

Rasputin lay unconscious on the coal pile for about thirty minutes. Suddenly he became aware of a bone-piercing coldness which was gripping him and sapping him of life. For the first time in many years, fear welled up in his soul as the finality of death bit into his consciousness, jarring him into sensitivity. He felt cold, so very cold. He could see nothing, but he could feel the crust of frozen blood on his cheeks. He tried to raise his head. Shots of pain darted down his spine. He was growing numb. He could not feel his left foot.

Slowly, gropingly, in the center of a fog of pain, he clawed his way to his feet. His knees wouldn't hold him. He had to crawl, using his arms to pull himself along. He stopped for a moment and rubbed his hands over his face to dislodge the clumps of blood. He felt nothing on the left side of his face. His right eye could discern only shadows. He saw the blue glimmer of moonlight on snow, a window.

He crawled over, mounted a barrel, and crawled out. He lay on his stomach, panting, enjoying the cold soft powder cooling his face. A stone wall faced him, about fifty meters away. He began slowly to advance on it, gaining power as he neared the last obstacle to his freedom. Only one thought obsessed his burning brain—escape, escape, escape.

He reached the wall, but it stood six feet high. Moving toward a stone bench that stood about twenty feet away, he could hear the low throaty growl of an animal coming from across the yard. He quickened his pace and heard the animals running in the snow. The dogs reached him as he gained the bench, yelping and snapping. More sounds, more running, human voices. He clawed his way up to the top of the wall. His fingers dug into the stones and he started to pull himself up. Hands clasped onto his legs, and in an instant he tumbled back onto the white ground.

He was possessed with pure, perfect, unconscious, animal rage. He lashed out. He grasped a head in his right hand and clutched at the warm throat. Warm blood; he wanted to bite but he was too weak. They subdued him. They trussed him up as a chicken, tied his hands behind him, brought him round back, and laid him in the back seat of a car.

They drove off, two of them in front and Rasputin in the back. Still he wasn't finished. He would outwit them. They had shot him and he had lived. They were fools. The ropes were loose. He would get them off now. Where was his left foot? He could not feel his left foot. No time for that now. The ropes. Get them off. There, now. One. Now the other. Stop now. Wait for them to stop.

The big black car approached the Neva River. A thick crust of glaucous ice sheeted the river from bank to bank. They drove over a bridge. The water welled up black and thick from the unfrozen crescents around the pillars of the base of the bridge. They stopped the car in an instant and were on him before he knew it. They heaved him, kicking over the rail and waited for the splash, then drove on.

Rasputin's body plunged down deep into the depths of the thick black water. He felt mad with desire. The coldness penetrated him; the pain drew him up, clawing and fighting. The pressure in his chest redoubled. His heart sent hammering shocks into his head. He must climb up. Something solid. There.

He hung onto the edge of the shelf of ice, and pulled in three or four deep breaths of air. It refreshed him. But the coldness penetrated his mind again; the wind bit into his head. The water numbed his legs. He pulled himself out of the water. Rest, rest, that's all he wanted now. But his mind revolted. Warmth, it said. Don't stop.

But it was no use. He was too tired. His body refused. He slipped and crunched into the ice and snow. He felt the cool receiving softness of the snow blanket. It was his last sensation before his spirit expired under the cold glittering eyes of the Russian night.

THIRTEEN

Simanovitsch and his son left Munia Golovina's house at about four-thirty. Semion went to get Protopopov; Simanovitsch to the police station nearest the Prince's palace. The chief of the precinct told him that the Prince's neighbors had reported hearing gunshots during the night. One woman reported hearing a high-pitched shriek, "Oh, God! Don't shoot him like that!"

Simanovitsch told the precinct chief he believed he knew who it was that they shot. The chief then remarked that he had a report from one of his own men that bore the same conclusion. This policeman reported that while he walked his beat a stranger came up to him in the night and said he was Purishkevitch, a delegate to the Duma, and that he had just killed Rasputin for the sake of all of Russia. The man looked drunk, however, so the policeman hadn't thought anything of it.

Simanovitsch instructed the chief to organize a citywide search for the body. Meanwhile, he decided to confront the Prince personally. He went to his palace and met him in the front salon. The Prince appeared pale and nervous, but otherwise showed no signs of any severe mental conflict.

"What have you done with Rasputin?" demanded Simanovitsch.

"We left him with the gypsies," said the Prince. "We drank with them and left about one. He stayed there with them."

"Shall you tell that to the Empress?" asked Simanovitsch. "She'll want to know what's become of her *starets*, you know. Is that what you'll say to her, Prince Yusupov? Will that be your lie?"

Yusupov didn't answer. He reached into his breast coat pocket and retrieved a small letter that recorded his claim of innocence. He handed it to Simanovitsch and said, "I have nothing more to say to you, Simanovitsch."

"I was wondering if perhaps you could explain to me, Prince," said the Jew, "how these blood stains got on your floor over there."

"One of my drunken guests shot a dog."

"I see," said Simanovitsch. He left.

Two days later, on his way back to police headquarters, the precinct chief met Semion and Protopopov. They said that they had found Rasputin's boot on a bridge over the Neva. All three returned to the bridge. They found a few drops of blood on the parapet of the structure. They descended down to the banks and combed the ice-sheet covering the river. Simanovitsch found a trail of blood leading away from the edge of the ice and followed it for about half a kilometer. They found the crumbled and frozen corpse around sunrise on January 1, 1917.

They removed the body to their car, transported it to the police station, and disbanded the search. Bishop Isidor was called in to administer the last rites. Then the body was moved to the Chesminskaya Chapel, between Tsarskoye Selo and St. Petersburg. Rasputin's daughters and nieces came with the materials to prepare the body. They washed the corpse and dressed it before the embalmers arrived.

The body was finally brought to the chapel at Tsarskoye Selo. Only the very close members of the Imperial circle attended the services. Bishop Pitirim was asked to conduct them, but he claimed that he was too shaken to do so. Bishop Isidor presided. The body was buried in a plot on the grounds of Tsarskoye Selo in a plain wooden casket with a plate of glass over the face of the deceased. A holy icon, dressed with the signatures of the Imperial Family, was placed on the dead peasant's chest. Alexis held the cross in the funeral procession; all of the Imperial Family participated in some way in the ceremony.

Alexandra took the event severely, shaking in pain and grief when she heard the news. Rasputin had been an integral pillar of support to her life. Now that it had been cut down, she felt weak, insecure, and alone. She and her daughters wept for days.

Nicholas was at headquarters when he heard the news of the assassination. Struck to the quick, he immediately set forth for home, giving orders that the ice on the Neva be broken from Kronstadt to St. Petersburg, an ancient Russian gesture of honor to a stricken hero. The gloom which descended on the Tsar was impenetrable. Neither the affairs of state nor the course of the war had much effect to his grief. He took Rasputin's death as an omen of an inevitable fate and simply let himself drift, more or less, until finally, in March, he was forced to abdicate the throne.

Apparently Rasputin had not been wholly insensitive to his own future. One day about nine months before his death, he had been possessed with a fit of excitement. He drank wine all day, bathed in the late afternoon, napped in the evening, and asked Simanovitsch to bring his friend, the attorney Aronson, over that night. When Aronson arrived, Rasputin sat him down and dictated his last will and testament.
Part of that document follows:

> . . . The spirit Grigori Yefimovitch Rasputin-Novitch, from the village of Pokrovskoye. I am writing and shall seal this letter in the city of St. Petersburg. I know that I shall leave this life within a year. I want to reveal to Papa, to the Russian Mother, and to the children of the Russian earth, what they should do.
>
> If Russian peasants, my brothers, should kill me, then you, Russian Tsar, need fear no one. Remain on your throne. In that case, take no cares on account of your children. They will reign throughout Russia for centuries.
>
> But if I am brought down by nobility, and they are the ones who shed my blood, their hands will remain soiled with my blood; for twenty-five years they will not get their hands clean. They will depart from Russia. Brother will rise up against brother and will murder each other, and in the course of twenty-five years, there will be no longer any nobility in the land.
>
> Tsar of the Russian nations; when you hear the tolling of the bells that announce to you the death of Grigori, so know that if any of your relatives have taken part in my death, then no one

from your family, that is, your children, or your relatives, will live longer than two years. The Russian people will kill them.

I am going away and I feel in myself God's instructions to tell the Russian Emperor how he should live after I disappear. You should reflect, consider everything, and act carefully. You should take care for your own salvation and tell your relatives that I have paid for them with my life. I will be killed. I am no more among the living. Pray, pray, pray. Be strong. Take care for yourself and for your family.

[Signed]
Grigori

Simanovitsch had taken the document for safekeeping; after the funeral, he brought it to the Imperial couple. Nicholas believed the prediction that his people would kill him. He discussed with Simanovitsch the last days of Rasputin's life, clinging to his memory, refusing to acknowledge the new situation.

Simanovitsch used his new-found influence to great purpose. The Tsar asked him if he knew of any minister who was implicated in the plot to kill Rasputin. Simanovitsch told him that Interior Minister Sukhomlinov and Justice Minister Maklakov both knew of the conspiracy but hadn't done anything about it one way or the other. Nicholas fired them both and asked Simanovitsch to name candidates to replace them. It was now that Simanovitsch convinced Nicholas that Dobrovolsky would do a fine job in the Justice Ministry and that General Belyayev was the man for the War Ministry. Both men were appointed the following day.

In their desire to keep alive the memory of their beloved *starets*, the Imperial couple decided to transform his home on Gorokhovaya Street into a national museum. Since this would obviously involve the relocation of Rasputin's daughters and nieces, Alexandra gave to Simanovitsch the sum of twelve thousand rubles to find them a new lodging. Some Polish friends of his owned a building at 13 Kollomenskaya, and he set them up in these rooms. The house cost him twenty-five thousand rubles.

Rasputin's daughters moved into their new home in dismay. Their old rooms had been done the way they had wanted them and these new ones caused them considerable discomfort. The girls had been accustomed to travel to Tsarskoye Selo to visit the daughters of the Tsarina; indeed, they were among the very few contacts these four sheltered Grand Duchesses had with the outer world and their appearance excited much interest among the Court. So the Tsarina noted their sadness even through the generally morose atmosphere of the bereaved Court.

The Imperial Family treated them with a special tenderness during these hard times. The Tsarina, for once breaking the habit of her parsimony, bought them each a fur coat. But true to her character, she purchased them on installment. When she saw the dismay in the girls' eyes over leaving their beloved home, she canceled her plans for the museum and paid out fifty thousand rubles to return the partly renovated building to its previous state.

The effect of the peasant's death on the Young Court was devastating. For the past few years Rasputin had been the source of energy for the Court. Who could take the place of such a vital being as Rasputin? Assuredly not Nicholas. No, the job of picking up the pieces fell to Protopopov. Everyone leaned on him, giving him the responsibilities of holding the reins of the shaking government while keeping the general populace below the point of insurrection.

But Protopopov had a long-standing feud with Rodzianko, the president of the Duma. One Sunday, during breakfast at Vyrubova's house, Simanovitsch and Vyrubova discussed this handicap and decided to go to Tsar Nicholas and convince him to arbitrate a reconciliation.

The next time that Rodzianko arrived at Tsarskoye Selo to report to Nicholas, the Tsar summoned Protopopov. The latter walked into Nicholas' office expecting a private interview, but found the Tsar engaged in conversation with the president of the Duma. Nicholas explained to both men how necessary it was to the integrity of the government that they cooperate with each other. But Rodzianko had his dander up; he refused to shake the proffered hand of the Interior Minister. Nicholas reddened, jumped up with his back to the obstinate president, and said to Protopopov, "Come, Interior Minister, there is nothing here for us."

Later that night Protopopov, in his best aristocratic style, sent his summons to Rodzianko to give him satisfaction. Then he telephoned Simanovitsch, informed him of the fiasco at Tsarskoye Selo, and announced the impending duel. Simanovitsch besought the Minister to desist from what could only result in further rifts in the already unsettled government. But Protopopov had made up his mind and would not retreat an inch.

Desperate, Simanovitsch called Alexandra, informed her of the duel, and begged her to intercede. Beside herself, the Empress called up Nicholas at headquarters and frantically related the news. Nicholas knew he had to do something, for he could afford neither to lose Protopopov nor to inflame the Duma, who would certainly blame the Tsar if Rodzianko fell. So he summoned Rodzianko to headquarters. The Duma president came expecting Nicholas to announce to him the creation of a cabinet responsible to the Duma. Instead Nicholas demanded that he refuse the upcoming duel.

Rodzianko returned to the capital in a rage, but in the morning Protopopov received a note from him. Unless Protopopov could produce a letter from Nicholas sanctioning the duel, the note said, Rodzianko would be obliged to refuse to accept the challenge. Of course, Nicholas refused Protopopov's request for such a letter. When Protopopov related these developments, Simanovitsch was so happy that he sent a case of champagne to each of the seconds to celebrate their not being needed.

During these months, antagonistic parties coalesced around the figures of Protopopov and Rodzianko. Stürmer was replaced as Minister-President by Vasili Trepov, whose allegiances were more with the Duma than with the Court. Nicholas had appointed him in the hopes of conciliating the fast-rising tempers of the representatives of the people, who had been becoming more and more vociferous after the assassination of Rasputin.

Trepov called a general meeting of the ministry, claiming that thenceforward all appointments to the ministry which the Tsar wished to make had to be approved by him. He called on Protopopov, Dobrovolsky, Belyayev, and Raja to hand him their resignations inasmuch as he did not approve of their presence in the ministry. Protopopov declared that, as far as he was concerned, he had been appointed by the Tsar, not the Duma, and that he owed allegiance to the Tsar alone. He refused to resign unless Nicholas asked him to. The others followed his example.

When Protopopov met Simanovitsch for dinner later that evening, he told him what the bold Trepov had endeavored to bring off. Simanovitsch frowned over his fish course and then said, "Scriblkantz, how would you like to resurrect the influence of Rasputin?"

"Resurrect the influence of Rasputin?" repeated the Interior Minister. "Why, whatever are you talking about, Simanovitsch?"

"Listen to me, my friend," said the Jew. "I have been thinking. I have a plan to bring back the influence of the *starets* on Nicholas."

"But how?" asked Protopopov.

"Rasputin was in the habit of scribbling his wishes down on scraps of paper. I happen to know that there are some men's names on such scraps who could be very useful to our cause if we could convince Nicholas to appoint them."

"But do you think Nicholas will believe you, Simanovitsch?"

"Well, he knows Rasputin's handwriting," said Simanovitsch. "All we have to do is find the scraps among his papers."

"Where are these?" asked the Minister.

"I have given some of them to Princess Sophia Tarkonova and some of them to Bishop Pitirim for safekeeping. I shall call on the Princess tonight."

Simanovitsch visited Princess Tarkonova later that night and perused the collection of Rasputin's manuscripts in her keeping. There was nothing of present value to him in the lot, so he bade her farewell.

The next morning he called on the Metropolitan Bishop and explained his plan to him. The Bishop agreed that the intrigue was necessary and gladly helped Simanovitsch sift through the unorganized mass of scraps, notes, letters, and documents. They were able to find four suitable names, and Simanovitsch left to meet Protopopov and tell him the news.

They resolved to go first to Vyrubova, a lady who exercised much weight with the Imperial Family in those days. She had accumulated a store of shared experiences with the Imperial Family, and they fell back on these now that their richer currents of life had ceased to flow.

Vyrubova usually shunned any entanglement in intrigue, refusing all who called on her to aid their cause. But when Simanovitsch presented a list to her of his candidates, asking her for her opinion of the quality of the men, and informing her that he had found the list among Rasputin's papers, the good woman was delighted to be thus connected to the deceased hero. She readily assented to help Simanovitsch by taking the list to the Tsarina.

Alexandra was extremely happy to receive it. Like Vyrubova she clutched at any straw that pretended to hold the aura of the departed *starets*. She summoned her special courier and charged him with delivering the list and her note directly to the Tsar, who was back at the front.

On receiving the list, Nicholas summoned Protopopov by telegram. When the Interior Minister arrived at headquarters, Nicholas showed him the list and asked him if he had any opinion of the candidates. Protopopov feigned surprise in seeing the piece of paper; he told the Tsar that he knew all the men and that they were extremely capable people.

The following day Trepov received notice of his dismissal, after only eight days in office. Nicholas replaced him with an old friend of Protopopov, the delightful Prince Golitsyn, whose surprise upon learning of his appointment compared only to that of the Duma, who had assumed Trepov's position was sacrosanct.

The Prince had found his way into Rasputin's notes by the efforts of his mistress. It seems she was the good friend of Protopopov's mistress, and when Protopopov's appointment ushered the pair into the larger realm of Imperial society, she had missed her confidante. Accordingly, she had gone to Rasputin and pleaded with him to raise up her Prince, so that once more she could receive the sisterly company of her more fortunate friend.

The other members of the new cabinet were Kochitsky, Minister for Cultural Affairs, Alexei Pokrovsky, Minister for Foreign Affairs, and Herder Boinovsky, the Transportation Minister. This new ministry promised to make life easier for Protopopov's party, but a few days after it took office, the Minister Protopopov approached

Simanovitsch with a long face. Dobrovolsky had brought up a proposal at the last Ministerial Council to have Simanovitsch exiled.

In short, Rasputin's former friend had too much power for Dobrovolsky's taste. He didn't enjoy the idea that a man who had pledged him eternal enmity as Simanovitsch had done after the Rubinstein affair, could within a week change the composition of half of the national cabinet.

Protopopov, of course, had stood up for his friend, reminding the Justice Minister that Aaron Simanovitsch had enjoyed the friendship of the Tsar of Russia for eleven years, and that this long-standing connection was especially dear to Nicholas, now that their mutual friend, the peasant, was gone. Dobrovolsky let it go at that.

Not only was the Young Court besieged by the representatives in the Duma, but the Old Court also pressed hard. For months now, the Imperial house's correspondence bristled with intrigue and plans of revolution. The letters fell under the scrutiny of the political police, so Nicholas at least knew who his enemies were. At banquets and balls, at theaters and opera houses, anywhere the Romanov family congregated, the whispers of dissatisfaction and conspiracy wafted through the air.

The most publicly mentioned conspiracy linked the Grand Duke Nicholas Mikhailovitch and the three sons of the late Grand Duke Vladimir—Cyril, Boris, and Andrew. They had decided upon a plan to declare Nicholas mentally incompetent, whereupon they would then exile Alexandra to a convent and declare the Grand Duke Nicholas Nicholaievitch regent to the Tsarevitch Alexis.

This plan was dropped in favor of the less dramatic, and more readily feasible, one proposed by the Dowager Empress Maria Feodorovna, who declared her willingness to ascend the throne herself and simply declare her son, the Grand Duke Michael Alexandrovitch, the Tsar of All the Russians.

Nicholas remained complacent while these rumors spread. The police kept him informed of the changing variations of the themes, but he just didn't care anymore. Rasputin's last testament had predicted not only his death, but that of all his family, even to his uncles and cousins. He placed full faith in this prophesy and therefore abandoned the Russian aristocracy to what seemed to him to be its inevitable fate. His days were clouded with a remorseless fatalism which crippled his spirit and suffused his will with its corrosive influence. The Tsar simply wondered when the debilitating civil war would commence.

The final and complete break between Nicholas and his family came in January 1917. Grand Duke Michael Alexandrovitch called upon the Empress to voice his dissatisfaction with the way they were handling the reins of government. Nicholas and his daughter Anastasia waited outside the bedroom where the ailing Empress conducted the audience. At one point the Grand Duke grew excited and expressed his sentiment in threatening terms. From his concealed position Nicholas listened to this outburst for only a moment and then marched into the room, cool and imperious.

This wholly unsettled his brother, who had thought Nicholas was at headquarters. Michael fumbled around, got flustered, and began to shout Nicholas down. The Tsar led him out of the palace and left word with the guard to eject any member of the Grand Duke's family who again sought entrance.

Vyrubova witnessed the whole scene from her post at Alexandra's bedside. Excusing herself from the presence of the upset Tsarina, she rushed to a telephone and rang Simanovitsch's number. She explained to him what had taken place and asked him to report the incident to Interior Minister Protopopov and request that he call her.

Rasputin had been in the habit of telephoning Alexandra at ten o'clock every night. They would discuss the day's events, the state of Alexis' health, and Court gossip. These conversations soothed the nerve-worn woman, giving her a daily source of sympathy and consolation to look forward to. Simanovitsch had been privy to the intimate relationship between Rasputin and the Empress and knew many of the small traditions which the Tsarina had learned to expect of these conversations. Since Rasputin's death, Protopopov had taken up the little ritual, trusting his friend to guide him through the fine points of these phone calls. Now Simanovitsch called the Interior Minister to advise him of the commotion at the palace and to urge him to call the Empress early.

The government of Russia went on in this quavering manner for only a few weeks more. The forces of revolution, which the Imperial Family itself had encouraged by its complicity in Rasputin's murder, multiplied themselves. The upper bourgeoisie, who were represented in the government by the delegates to the Duma, became steadily more fierce, and the Old Court realized it was losing to them the central focus of revolutionary agitation. By March the situation in the capital reached the threshold of chaos.

Protopopov and the leaders of the garrisons miscalculated the latent energies that had built up over months of uncertainty, and years of war and suffering. Because they agreed with Nicholas that any risk was necessary to bring the war to a speedy conclusion, they decided to put through the plan to stage a mock insurrection, believing they could handle the crowds and any after effects which the paid rabble-rousers could initiate.

But the plan backfired: when they released their fictitious demonstration, all hell broke loose. The fury of years of frustration came weltering to the surface, spilling wave upon wave of dissatisfied and determined workers into the streets. The crowds burst through the military dikes and swarmed through the public buildings. Protopopov cabled Nicholas that the situation was rapidly getting out of his control and advised the Tsar to hurry back from the front.

Nicholas immediately set out by train. Cables reached him hourly recording the disintegration of his government. The Duma and the Soviets were riding the crest of the wave of fury. Communications had been seized, printing offices were taken, and the garrisons switched allegiances to the side of the revolutionaries. Finally, his own cherished palace guard fell away from the crumbling Tsar.

Nicholas urgently telegraphed his generals, spread out over three fronts and three thousand miles of battlegrounds, informing them of the situation in the great cities and requesting their advice. The responses came back unanimously. Grand Duke Nicholas Nicholaievitch's answer typified their feelings. It read: ABDICATE.

Even if Nicholas had decided to buck this concensus and rally his forces, he never had the chance to fight back. For as the Imperial train coasted through the station of Pskov, a delegation from the Duma halted its progress and boarded it with drawn weapons to demand the Tsar's abdication. At first Nicholas thought to abdicate in favor of his son Alexis. But his paternal feelings rebelled, for he surely would have been separated from the boy if he made him Tsar, and he couldn't bear that. So he passed on his crown to his brother Michael.

Grand Duke Michael Alexandrovitch heard the news in shock. He hadn't ever dreamed that the burdens of state leadership would fall on his shoulders. He couldn't believe the heir to the throne had been bypassed. He went to the capital where, in the midst of chaos, he inquired of Rodzianko whether the Duma could give him any guarantees for his welfare. Rodzianko replied that he could give no guarantee. The Grand Duke thought for five minutes, then signed the second abdication document on March 16, 1917. After three hundred and four years of rule, the House of Romanov—and with it, the Russian monarchy—had been swept away.

FOURTEEN

Simanovitsch's first encounter with the martial forces of the Revolution occurred a few days after Nicholas' abdication. A band of soldiers came up to his house and demanded that he tell them the whereabouts of Ministers Protopopov and Stürmer. When he feigned ignorance, they entered the premises, roughly searched the place, and left in a huff without their quarry.

Princess Tarkonova appeared the next day with the inevitable news: The Minister of Justice of the Provisional Government, Alexander Kerensky, had ordered Simanovitsch's exile from St. Petersburg. Simanovitsch thanked her for the information, but told her that he didn't think he was quite ready to leave the capital. He wanted to stay around until the general drift of events became more clear. She prevailed upon him, however, to move out of his house, and he registered at a small hotel under the name of Shikmanovitch.

After two quiet days, his vigil was interrupted. A young fellow by the name of Buchanan, a student for whom Simanovitsch had obtained admission to law school, led into the hotel a bunch of soldiers who marched up to his room and broke down the door. Buchanan drew his revolver and announced that Simanovitsch was under arrest by order of the President of the Provisional Government.

They packed Simanovitsch into a truck with other enemies of the new state and brought them to an army barracks. Later they transferred Simanovitsch to a guarded room in the Alexander Nevsky Monastery where Protopopov and Stürmer had also been deposited. In the morning all three were driven to the Imperial Duma. With a huge crowd swarming all about this huge building, the prisoners were hustled inside and thrust into a jammed room where most of the high officials of the Tsar's government had been stored.

There was shouting, pushing, shoving, and general uproar in the room. Simanovitsch demanded to know the charges which were raised against him, saying that he had merely engaged in his trade, that of Court jeweler; on occasion he had aided his Jewish brethren. Was this cause for incarceration, he demanded? But his cries fell on indifferent ears. Apparently the favors which he had dispensed were now being defined as criminal actions.

Soon they brought him into another, less crowded room. He found among the prisoners the daughters of Rasputin and his own sons and wife. They also had been arrested by students whom he had once helped. Cyril Markov III and Dimitri Rupensky, both delegates to the Duma, presided over the room. Lying on a table was a pile of gems that Simanovitsch realized had been taken from a safe in his house. Semion demanded that a receipt be drawn up, numbering each of the articles, but Rupensky sneered at him and had him removed from the room, remarking that the jewels had been confiscated.

During the night, various revolutionary officials interrogated Simanovitsch concerning his life in the Court of Nicholas. They wanted to know all about Rasputin, the peasant's relations to the Imperial Family, his intimate home life, and details of similar nature. Simanovitsch persisted that he himself was but a simple Court jeweler, a businessman who quietly plied his trade and went home when the day was done, asking no questions and generally minding his own business.

Upon hearing of the arrest of Simanovitsch and his family, Attorney Sliosberg, who had worked with him on the affair involving the sugar manufacturers, immediately set about gaining their release. He went to Kerensky first and informed him that inasmuch as none of the family were officials of the previous government, he could detain them only as witnesses, not as prisoners. In the morning Simanovitsch's family were released, but not Simanovitsch himself: he had gotten himself involved in an incident.

In the early morning the Grand Duke Cyril had marched at the head of a division of Marines to the steps of the Duma to declare his support of the new regime. His advent was cheered and applauded by the crowd. In the height of the feverish saluting, a delegate from the Duma ascended a table in the room where Simanovitsch was situated and roundly denounced the previous government, hailing the abdication of Nicholas as the most glorious achievement since Napoleon had been driven from Russian soil. His shouts were drowned by the jeers of the captives. Ink, bottles, shoes, papers, and books were hurled on the poor man. Simanovitsch lent a hand in the fracas, the guards singled him out as a perpetrator, and he was shipped off to the dingy, dank fortress of Saints Peter and Paul.

Meanwhile, his two sons fanned out and contacted all of the Jewish politicians who held positions in the new government. But whether Simanovitsch had helped them or not, they shied away from him now, reluctant to be tagged as his friend; they didn't want to hear anything about his plight. Finally one of them helped Semion and Jacob get their father transferred to the more humane quarters of the Kresty prison.

Simanovitsch received two visitors in his new quarters. The first, Justice Minister Peraversev, came to him with a haughty air of snobbery. He hadn't had the time as yet to draw up Simanovitsch's indictment, but he told him not to fret, he would get to it just as soon as he could. Simanovitsch wanted to kick Peraversev as he left the cell, but he restrained himself, having learned that one doesn't tempt one's victors.

His second visitor brought him better news. The Attorney Feidelson told him that he had secured Simanovitsch's transfer to the Arresting House, where there was every chance that his freedom would be obtained. After he was transported there, he quickly sought out the right people and deposited with them a voucher for two hundred thousand rubles—the sum was to be paid to Peraversev. It hurt Simanovitsch's pride to have to be the agent of the snide Justice Minister's enrichment, but he could not tolerate confinement; he wasn't a man who could survive in a cage. It was the pain of parturition; Simanovitsch walked freely the next day.

After assuring himself of the safety of his own family, his first concern was with the Imperial Family. After the abdication, Nicholas had been sent to Tsarskoye Selo and placed under house arrest. The revolutionaries sent the famous palace guard away, replaced them with their own regiment, and released all of the ground attendants and all the domiciliary personnel down to the barest level, leaving the Tsar to a life of extreme humility, at the mercy of the revolutionaries.

Simanovitsch, realizing that if the Tsar were to be rescued, he would not be able to remain inside the country, quietly set out to Germany to discuss the situation with Kaiser Wilhelm. The Royal Houses of Germany, England, and Russia pulsed with the same royal blood through the venerable Queen Victoria. Simanovitsch figured to invoke this connection in the court of the Kaiser, who after all was the Tsar's cousin.

When he arrived in Berlin once again and began sniffing the air for its secrets, Simanovitsch found, to his relief, that plans to rescue the Romanovs had been flying off the Teutonic drawing boards in droves. Every conceivable modality of escape had been explored. The Kaiser cogitated in his secret basement, his great busy countenance furrowed hard over the wealth of possibilities before him, sifting and screening the merely fantastical from the fallible, the chancy from the extravagant, the imaginative from the plausible.

On the eve of his appointed audience with the Kaiser, Simanovitsch got little sleep. He had never met Wilhelm, but he had heard all the legends swirling about the awesome name. Even his close association with the rarefied atmosphere of the magnificent Russian Court made a poor shield against these anxieties which the morrow's audience engendered.

But the meeting went off splendidly. The Kaiser had been sinking under the sheer elaboration of the many plots which his staff produced. Even that morning a factory in Dresden had begun the manufacture of seven plastic dummies, molded in the exact likenesses of Nicholas and his family. Simanovitsch's plan was so simple it brought smiles.

"Well, Mr. Aaron Simanovitsch, so you have come to see me about your poor caged Tsar," snorted the Kaiser, barely looking up from his paper-mounded desk. "Speak. What do you wish to say to me. Be quick."

"Your Majesty," began Simanovitsch, "I apologize for intruding on you at this time, but my concern for Nicholas, your cousin"—Simanovitsch stressed this word ever so much more than he had to—"has given me courage to bring my humble words to your ear. Most Imperial Majesty, my country falters under the burdens of this war. She must seek an end to the hostilities. But if you demanded, in a secret, secondary clause to any peace treaty, the transfer of Nicholas to your land, our present government would have to acquiesce. The risks of rescue can be obviated by negotiation. It can happen very easily: Russia must end this war, for she is bleeding and bankrupt."

The Kaiser looked at Simanovitsch open-mouthed. The idea had never occurred to him to make Nicholas' rescue a condition of a peace treaty. He smiled.

"Mr. Simanovitsch," he returned, "you are a credit to your race. Now you must excuse me—I have work to do. What you suggest shall be considered gravely. It's simplicity is admirable. Yes, I shall think of it seriously. Good morning." And with this clipped response, the peremptory Kaiser ushered Simanovitsch out of his august presence.

With the happy belief that Nicholas' escape would be guaranteed in any possible peace treaty, Simanovitsch made the journey back across the plains of eastern Europe to St. Petersburg.

However, after a few days in the chaotic capital, Simanovitsch realized the great danger he risked in returning. Events in the political area proceeded by staggering leaps and bounds. He decided to move to Kiev, bringing his family and most of his hard cash. But there was one last precaution he had to see to before his departure. Carrying one million rubles in cash and one thousand carats of gems, he called a friend who practiced medicine. His friend obligingly put these items—and Simanovitsch's left arm—into a plaster cast.

During his subsequent trip Simanovitsch was searched many times—twice in Moscow itself—but no one discovered the cache.

He arrived with his family in Kiev during the hetman regime. Simanovitsch was met at the station by his brother Akazatov. There was great excitement in the reunion, but his brother's agitation was mingled with concern. One of Aaron's arch enemies had been in town; Vladimir Purishkevitch, one of the architects of Rasputin's murder, had been nosing around, searching for the Jew, boasting that when he found him he would kill him.

Simanovitsch went directly to Count Keller, the head of the Northern Army, who was presently camped outside the city, and whom Simanovitsch had helped many times in better days. His plea for aid won him the protection of a military guard which the Count offered freely and with alacrity, as a way of returning former favors. He sent Simanovitsch to General Zeveloshsky, commander of the B division of the army, who invited Simanovitsch to join up with him.

The Northern army had been cut off from the rest of the forces, however, and the General had to contend with both a severe disciplinary problem and an almost impossible logistical one. The Southern army, with which Purishkevitch had been affiliated, had been permitting its troops to loot and plunder. General Zevoloshsky's sensibilities raised him above that sort of barbarism, but he had no food, and he asked Simanovitsch to help solve the dilemma. He guaranteed that he would keep his troops out of the Jewish ghettoes if only Simanovitsch could feed them.

Combining her predilictions with his practical experience, Simanovitsch found an elegant solution. Under military protection, he opened a casino in Kiev which catered to the needs of the officers of three armies in the area, to the rich refugees, and to the upper class of the city itself. The establishment quickly netted Simanovitsch ten thousand pounds sterling per day.

With this money Simanovitsch was able to help many of the less fortunate refugees by offering them a daily free lunch. Heartened, he made the rounds of all the more fortunate among the refugees and collected another six million rubles for the division. In gratitude, General Zevoloshsky ordered that the Jews who had been drafted in the national conscription be organized into units which would be sent into the suburbs to protect the Jewish communities.

At this point General Belyayev, the former War Minister, arrived in Kiev. Over lunch at the casino he gave Simanovitsch the news that Purishkevitch was again on his way to the city, traveling with two officers from the Southern army, to fulfill their desire to wreak vengeance on the Jews for having incited the revolution.

The Russian Jewish community had been blamed for getting Russia into the Great War, they had been blamed for the defeats Russia suffered during the course of the war, and now they were being blamed for the oncoming revolution! Purishkevitch had hopes of inciting a pogrom in the suburb of Podol, the site of an especially large Jewish population.

Simanovitsch sent an armed guard of two hundred soldiers to the threatened city with orders to find Purishkevitch and see that he left in short order. When the troops reached the city, Purishkevitch's delegate had succeeded only in igniting the tempers of the citizenry but no physical damage had been done. The guard restored peace to the town and on the second day of their presence in Podol, Purishkevitch complied with their command to depart.

But danger was never far away in such unsettled times. The Tetulyuras were bands of Cossacks which had been running throughout the plains of the Ukraine, terrorizing the cities and villages. When they gathered together their forces in the fall, they decided to attack Kiev. Taking the city after five days of bloody battle, they found Count Keller in a hotel room and led him out to the main street to be shot. They ransacked the town, looting, raping, and murdering at will. Simanovitsch and General Zevoloshsky managed to escape, but they lost the division's food fund. The trunk containing the money had been too weighty and bulky to travel with them on their swift flight.

When they reached Odessa, they decided to separate and stay at different hotels. Simanovitsch stayed at the Victoria, the General at the Commercial. Since Simanovitsch had retained his plaster cache, he had his own source of money and soon cultivated the reputation of being a great spender. One night his notoriety almost caused a catastrophe.

His face lathered, he was standing before the mirror in his hotel room in the process of shaving before dinner, when suddenly the door crashed open. He spun around to face two swarthy youths with bandanas around their necks and hand grenades in their hands. The hairier of the two demanded fifteen thousand rubles. Simanovitsch went calmly over to his bureau and found himself a towel with which he began to wipe his face.

He asked the two robbers if they were of the infamous band led by Mishka Yaponshik and, if so, whether they were acting on behalf of their leader or on their own. They were nonplussed by the Jew's calm handling of the situation. When Simanovitsch mentioned to them his friendship with Belyayev and his knowledge of Yaponshik's relation to the good General, they opened their mouths in awe. No one was supposed to be privy to the affiliation of the bandit and the General! Simanovitsch gave each young man three hundred Ukrainian rubles and packed them on their way, sending his good wishes to their leader.

That night he went to a nightspot he knew of through Alexander Fishon, who had been helped by Simanovitsch when he was organizing the St. Petersburg Jewish theater company and who was a friend of the owner, an actor. Simanovitsch spied Belyayev and Rashevsky at another table and decided to join them. They drank the night away. Toward dawn, all three decided to leave together. Rashevsky got a drashka to carry them back to their several hotels. During the ride, to Simanovitsch's astonishment, Belyayev took out his gun and shot Rashevsky four times in the chest. The General explained that Rashevsky had been a member of the conspiracy against Rasputin and that he had just paid him for that duplicity.

Simanovitsch suspected that there was more to it than that. A few nights later, while he was dining, two of Yaponshik's men came up to his table and asked him if he knew where Belyayev could be found. Simanovitsch pointed over his shoulder to the bar where Belyayev stood drinking. The two men took him outside. Simanovitsch heard two shots, ran outside, saw the General's body in a heap on the street, got a drashka, and took him to the hospital.

The wounds weren't fatal, and during his convalescence, the General told Simanovitsch the true story. He had shot Rashevsky for plotting with Yaponshik against him. His bullet wounds bespoke the latter's vengeance.

One day, Simanovitsch sat enjoying lunch with several of his

"The Dissolute One"

Grigori Rasputin, Bishop Hermogen, and the monk Iliodor

Rasputin convalescing after an assassination attempt on the eve of the First World War.

The Emperor Nicholas II and his cousin, the Grand Duke Nicholas Nicholaievitch, one of the realm's most virulent anti-Semites. The Emperor succeeded him as Commander-in-Chief of the Army, following pressure from Rasputin and Simanovitsch.

Prince Felix Yusupov, one of Rasputin's assassins, and his wife, Princess Irina Yusupov, the Emperor's only niece.

The Yusupov Palace on the Moika Canal, St. Petersburg

The room in the Yusupov Palace in which Rasputin was assassinated.

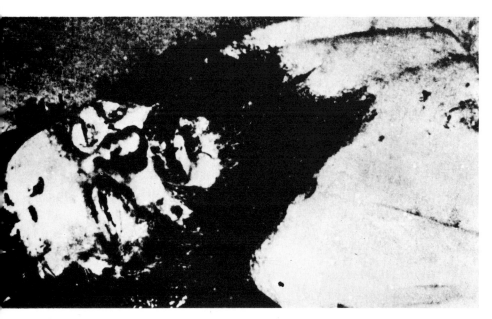

Rasputin's corpse after its recovery from the frozen banks of the Neva River.

The Tsar of All the Russians during his imprisonment at Tsarskoye Selo.

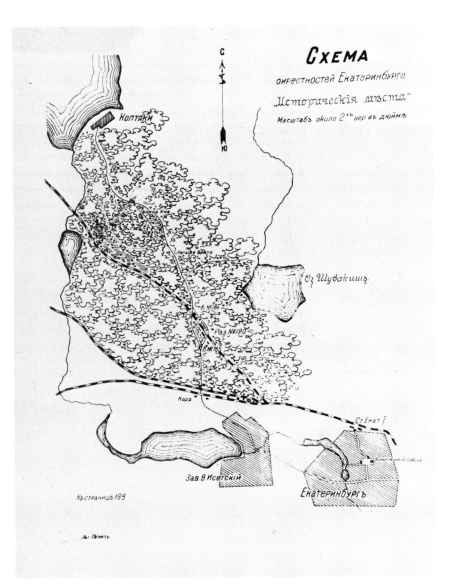

Къ страницѣ 198

Лит Печать

A map of Ekaterinburg in Siberia and the surrounding area

The Ipatiev House at Ekaterinburg

The room in the Ipatiev House where Nicholas II and his family were thought to have been "assassinated."

friends, Prince Nisharadze, General Zevoloshsky, and General Markov Modell. Abruptly, Simanovitsch saw the figure of Purishkevitch enter the doorway. He drew his gun and rested it on his knee under the table. Apparently Purishkevitch perceived Simanovitsch with an equal dose of surprise, for he hung fire for a moment, not quite knowing what he should do. Finally he decided to approach, but as he neared the table Prince Nisharadze accosted him and immediately warned him off, saying, "Purishkevitch, if you so much as lay one finger on Simanovitsch, I shall kill you."

"My dear Prince," said the suave former delegate, "you do me great injustice in attributing such warlike sentiments to me. Why, it has been ages since I desired this good man's skin."

"Aye," Zevoloshsky put in, "and it's been ages since you walked in that door and saw him with his friends, I suppose?"

"Why, you too, kind General?" asked Purishkevitch, "Well, by all rights I should turn around and march out of here without conducting the business with my good Jewish friend that I have come here to conclude."

"That's right," said the Prince. "In executing that plan, you would do wonders for your health."

"But, gentlemen," Purishkevitch purred, "I shall disregard your too common uncivilities, for I expect them from such as you— forgive me, Simanovitsch, I *do* mean to exclude you from that statement."

"What is all this fawning coming to?" said Simanovitsch, speaking for the first time.

"My friend, I wish to forge our reconciliation. Betokening my sentiment, I wish you would do me the honor to accept these." Purishkevitch handed Simanovitsch an envelope. "They are fifty seats on the steamship *Prodigal* departing tomorrow for Novorossiisk. Bon voyage!"

Purishkevitch bowed and left.

Simanovitsch was shocked. He didn't know what to think. Not for a moment did he believe the sentiments which his enemy had just expressed, but life here in Odessa was depressing him. He decided to risk the trip. Accordingly, he gathered together his sons and guard and went out the next morning in search of the *Prodigal*. He spied the ship moored about five hundred yards offshore and hired a launch to transport his entourage and baggage out to it.

Aboard the steamer, he quickly sought out the captain, checked his tickets, and then supervised the stowing of his gear. By noon his affairs were settled, the men had moved into their quarters, and Simanovitsch set out to reconnoiter the vessel. To his satisfaction he found that the majority of the men on board were either retired monarchists, police officials, or guards. He was beginning to entertain the idea that Purishkevitch might be human after all.

But his innate caution—and, indeed, the situation itself—never allowed him to slip so far as to rest complacently. As soon as the great ship began to make headway, the deck bulged with an excited crowd of young men from whom Simanovitsch could pick up murmurings of a seafaring pogrom. Three young journalists found themselves surrounded by the crowd. None of them were Jews, but the men believed that two of them looked like they were and that the third deserved to be treated like one because his brother had been a member of the Bolshevik party.

Simanovitsch, who with his two sons comprised the total Jewish population on board, became worried. He sent them to call up the bodyguard while he himself went to the rescue of the besieged journalists. As he approached the ugly knot of men, he listened to the projected plans; they wanted to throw the two suspected Jews into the water and shoot the other man.

Simanovitsch drew his pistol and fired two shots in the air. His decisive authority quickly separated the crowd and made a way for him up the center of the gathering.

By the time Simanovitsch had reached the leaders, his armed men had surrounded the crowd. He pointed this out to the officers and inquired as to the substance of the altercation between the three men and the inflamed group. Of course, substantive reason could be offered for the proposed execution. Simanovitsch asked the journalists how much money they had. Fifteen hundred pounds, they said. Simanovitsch had them distribute three thousand francs and five hundred pounds to the leaders of the group. The crowd broke up, and the voyage was completed with no further incidents.

The day after Simanovitsch arrived in Novorossiisk, the city celebrated the return of the well-known General Schurov. They still looked upon him as a commander even if he no longer had any forces to command. Only two trumpeters were left over from the whole army. The Rumanian violinist Gulesco's band traded turns with a gypsy choir in singing the city's sentiments for the army hero and the citizenry arranged a dinner in his honor. During the festive meal, the General bespoke his wish that the merchants raise two hundred million rubles for him so that he could re-equip an army and set out again against the Bolsheviks.

The merchants and financiers who attended the party received the General's proposition with interest. There was much talk of how to proceed to raise the sum. But during the wee hours of the morning, when the celebration reached its full, the General let fall a remark which tarnished his once bright chances for a comeback. He had complained to someone about the ingratitude of his Cossack soldiers. He had allowed them to loot and pillage the civilian population, but after they had thus enriched themselves, they had given up the fight against the Bolsheviks and dispersed into their villages and hamlets. Only the Rumanian bands and the gypsies had remained faithful to him. This illustration of the character of the General's discipline threw a wet blanket on the merchants' plans. Not one ruble was ever raised.

Soon after, General Mamontov arrived in Novorossiisk. His fame had preceded him as a vicious enemy of the Bolshevik forces. In his inimitable style, Simanovitsch managed to become friends with him and learned that the General was carrying a great deal of money which he had just reaped from his last campaign. Naturally Mamontov didn't want anyone to find out about it, and he asked Simanovitsch if he knew anyone who dealt in gems.

Simanovitsch knew that many of the wealthy Kiev sugar manufacturers who had fled to Novorossiisk had brought their jewels with them. He asked the General to trust him with the money, and Mamontov handed over a million rubles. Simanovitsch hid them in a shop owned by his friend Benjamin Feldman. Then Simanovitsch let it be known that he was once more in business. Manufacturers flocked to him to sell their gems. Simanovitsch returned to Mamontov with a million rubles worth of jewelry, purchased at bargain prices. At this stage the General told Simanovitsch that the chief reason he wanted this to be kept quiet had to do with a promise he had made to his men to cut them in on the profits of the campaign. Mamontov intended to break that promise.

Simanovitsch listened to the General's confession in silence. Although he acted as if he were in complete sympathy with the General's design, he started to keep an eye out for him. Later in the week he learned from one of his men that Mamontov not only had cash, but had brought with him a train wagon full of gold and silver objects garnered from the civilians he had supposedly protected.

One day, two of Mamontov's officers, tired of waiting for their General to make good on his promises, decided to take things into their own hands and burst into Simanovitsch's room demanding to be told the whereabouts of the General's valuables. Simanovitsch wasn't about to divulge the cache, as in all probability Feldman's shop would be wrecked in the aftermath of a search. There was a struggle. Simanovitsch wrestled one man to the door and tore the pistol out of his hands, knocking him out with it. His bodyguard heard the ruckus and came in just as the second officer was about to repay Simanovitsch. They brought both men before the City Commander, who listened to their grievance and mediated the case. The General's goods were finally dispersed among the eligible troops.

After this incident Purishkevitch again found his way into Simanovitsch's life. Simanovitsch came across a pamphlet selling in a nightclub for fifteen rubles entitled, "The Murder of Rasputin." The document reeked of anti-Semitism and flaunted flagrant lies. Simanovitsch bought up every pamphlet and waited around for the publisher—who appeared to be Purishkevitch—to show up to collect his profit.

Simanovitsch stayed just long enough to make sure the man knew who had foiled him. On the way home, with his bodyguard, he encountered a band of armed thugs. In the contest one of the thugs was killed; the others fled. Simanovitsch complained to the authorities, with whom he had been on excellent terms, and Purishkevitch was exiled.

Puishkevitch returned a month later, however. This time he attracted attention with his bill advertising a public lecture he planned to give. Simanovitsch smiled, assured that it was but one more scheme to incite the citizens against the Jews. Purishkevitch's tactics were nothing if not thorough.

At that time in Novorossiisk one of the local celebrities was a sailor by the name of Batkin who possessed that peculiar and rare quality of oratorical rhetoric which could sweep a crowd and bring it to a collective resolution in an instant. Simanovitsch hired him to speak against Purishkevitch on the same day as his scheduled lecture. On the day of battle Simanovitsch gathered his men together and swelled Purishkevitch's audience. Before the lecturer could spout one word of abuse, Simanovitsch and his men had shouted and stoned him out of the city.

But this still wasn't the last Simanovitsch saw of him. A little later the unhappy exile returned to the city, afflicted with a case of typhus he picked up in some unsanitary provincial pleasure-house. Unwittingly, the sick Purishkevitch admitted himself to the one hospital in the city which, except for the nursing care, was staffed entirely by Jews. The institution's nursing was handled by the Sisters of Mercy, a fiercely monarchistic religious order which had been furious at Purishkevitch for his complication in the recent conspiracies. It was rumored that Purishkevitch died in the hospital, but Simanovitsch never knew whether his enemy died a natural death.

While Simanovitsch had been passing his time in southern Russia, Nicholas and Alexandra had been shipped to eastern Russia. They had often heard from Rasputin about the lands east of the Urals as he discoursed ad infinitum about the vicissitudes of life in his childhood village. Now at last—but hardly in the best of conditions—the Imperial Family had a chance to see his cherished vistas.

The summer after the March Revolution, the Imperial train carried the dethroned monarch, his family, and his portable wealth to the Siberian town of Tobolsk. They were treated well enough there; the governor of the province vacated his mansion for them, and the garrison of soldiers surrounding them kept at a respectful distance. But for the man who had been the richest person in the world, the modesty of his new life may have tasted bitter. At least his beloved family was together, and the situation was bearable.

There were many, many Russians who stood to gain a fortune if they could free the Imperial Family from their Siberian bondage. Countless rescue operations were formulated all over Russia. The peace treaty with Germany had not yet been negotiated, and the German efforts hadn't been made public. Thus, many citizens scrambled to accept the challenge. An underground monarchistic organization was formed in the town of Tiumen, near Tobolsk, to coordinate these efforts, but curiously, none of the attempts went forward to execution. The reason lay in the ignominious work of Boris Soloviev.

Soloviev was the son of an official in the Holy Synod. He had attended the gymnasium in Kiev and when the war struck he received a promotion to officer. After the Revolution he found himself blessed: his friend Guchkov became War Minister.

But even before this event, the young officer had planned his future well. His scheme for success was very cleverly interwoven with the Imperial Family's troubled situation. An artist of dissimulation, Soloviev knew all about the close intimacy between Rasputin's daughters and the Imperial Family. He approached Maria with nothing but solicitude and concern. The troubled girl learned to find solace in his presence and when he proposed marriage in the fall of 1917, she accepted. They exchanged their vows in September.

In January of 1918 he traveled to Tiumen to effect his plan. Establishing himself in a bakery in Tobolsk, he communicated with the Imperial Family by sending notes to them in their bread. As Maria's husband, he gained their confidence and soon began mediating their correspondence with the outside world. Being both baker and postmaster proved a lucrative trade, for Nicholas sent out large amounts of cash to be deposited in foreign banks or handed over to various friends to underwrite rescue attempts. Needless to say, Soloviev appreciated much of this.

He soon infiltrated the monarchists' own underground. To all those who voiced their plans to rescue Nicholas, Soloviev had the same reply: Wait, I shall be the one to act first; the time isn't yet ripe. Those who failed to heed his advice found time to measure the truth of his words; each of them was arrested by government agents before he could complete even the preliminary stages of his plans.

Soloviev had good connections with the War Ministry; soon everyone believed him.

His position swayed tenuously under the Bolshevik regime, however. He knew it would all come falling down one day if he tempted fate. So he made the best of it while he dared, tempering his greed with his common sense and, after a time, called it quits, traveling east to the port of Vladivostok, from where he embarked for Paris.

FIFTEEN

On March 3, 1918, in the town of Brest-Litovsk, the seat of the German headquarters for the Eastern Front, a delegation of Bolsheviks signed the peace treaty with Germany. The Germans had driven a hard bargain: all the lands conquered by Russia since the time of Peter the Great reverted either to independence or to German sovereignty. The Russian empire lost the energies of sixty million souls.

Nicholas, in Tobolsk, wept when he learned of the humiliating agreement. But he couldn't feel wholly dejected about the document, for with the signing of it he and his family obtained their freedom. The Kaiser had succeeded in inserting the secret clause; it was now a matter of days until they would be at liberty. The family huddled together in anticipation, surreptitiously preparing.

But the days dragged on, the weeks came and went. No sign appeared. Another week, and then still another. The order for the move never came.

Since Purishkevitch's death Simanovitsch had been living easily in Novorossiisk, enjoying the flashy life of the city and breathing in the effulgence of the spring blossoms. One day he came into the hotel from his early morning walk and went to the desk to pick up his mail. There was a packet of letters and two or three telegrams. He went out to the back garden, ordered his coffee, and began browsing through the missives.

A cable from Moscow startled him out of his cozy nonchalance. One of his agents had sent it, not bothering in his urgency to encode the information. It read,

SOVIET PREPARING IMPERIAL TRIAL. NICHOLAS AND FAMILY IN GRAVE DANGER. STILL AT TOBOLSK. WILL LEAVE FOR HERE NEXT WEEK.

So the Bolsheviks had gone back on their promise, taking their chances and staging a dramatic trial and execution for propaganda purposes. Realizing that their psychological hold on the people of Russia could be tightened immeasurably by the destruction of these potent symbols of prerevolutionary Russia, the Bolsheviks were willing to gamble that Wilhelm wouldn't send back an army now, when he was so pressed on the Western Front.

Simanovitsch had to work fast. He had at his disposal less than one week, in which time a rescue had to be created, coordinated, and executed. He left for Tiumen immediately.

When he arrived he went straight to the monarchist headquarters. The place had been turned topsy-turvy in the wake of Soloviev's departure and the subsequent uncovering of his misdeeds. Though he was shocked at their disarray, Simanovitsch pulled the ranks together.

"How could a treacherous little weasel like that dishearten fifty grown men!" he exclaimed.

No one could answer him; they just winced at the sting of his sarcasm. He set them to work, and in two days he had all the information he needed to plan his greatest achievement. And it was so simple!

Yakovlev, an ambitious local commissar, was the engineer of the Imperial train. Simanovitsch gave him fifty thousand rubles to assure his cooperation. They would simply reroute the train from Moscow to the German border. Nothing could appeal to Simanovitsch's practical mind more than this so essentially simple stratagem.

The whole line from Tobolsk to Moscow had to be paved with bribes, but these proved easy enough to lay down. The railroad men were willing; they had merely to prevaricate for a few hours, after which they could call in the delay. It would not matter then to the success of the mission, since no one would know where the train was. A night's journey over the Ukrainian plains would whisk the Tsar into freedom.

As the train eased out of the local station in the rosy, Siberian dawn, it carried only three of the seven prisoners, Nicholas, Alexandra, and Maria. Alexis had been ill and his three other sisters remained in Tobolsk to care for him. These four would be sent for later. The ride progressed in tense silence with just the insistent chug-chug of the train rattling into the morning stillness. The trip seemed interminable, and it took twenty hours to reach the western plains.

Simanovitsch waited in Germany. He had crossed the border during the night, after having laid down the last bribe in the last Russian town. But the train never showed up; something had gone amiss. He hurried to the telegraph office to cable for news.

Just at the last hour, the Bolsheviks had discovered the renegade train. They sealed off the border and sent the train back to Siberia until an investigation could be made. They sent a new regiment with a new commander to sit over the Imperial captives and hustled out the local gentleman from his mansion on one day's notice.

The Imperial Family's new home took on the name of its former owner, Ipatiev House. It nestled in the valley of Ekaterinburg.

Simanovitsch got this news during the week from cables sent him by his agents. Crestfallen but determined, he set forth into Germany to reach the Kaiser and resurrect Wilhelm's old desire to save his kin.

When he arrived in Berlin, he spent a few days getting settled. He sent in his card to the Imperial secretary and found himself reunited with the glaring Prussian monarch. By this time the meeting comprised a threesome. A man who called himself Charles James Fox shared Simanovitsch's audience.

Fox, a genuine New Englander, as he fervently reiterated at least thrice a day, had been sent as the most trusted agent of George V of England. The verve of the polyglot Yankee startled Simanovitsch. But he had had relations with Americans before in his jewelry business, and while he had never yet been thrust up so near a specimen of the new world's keen race, he had been given in these dealings a foretaste of the pleasures which such an experience now afforded him.

Fox had informed the Kaiser that George V aspired to achieve the rescue of his relative Nicholas, and that the British Crown would personally pick up any expenses incurred in the exploit, no matter how large they might be. The Kaiser's steely gray eyes twinkled. Of course, he would be perfectly willing to accommodate His Majesty. The Kaiser charged Fox and Simanovitsch with execution of the deed, told them that the mannikins which he had had made up in his cousins' likenesses lay waiting in a warehouse in Dresden, and sent them away to do what they could.

Simanovitsch and Fox dined together after their interview. If they were going to work together on the rescue, then they felt they ought to spend as much time as they could in conjunction, as the job which lay ahead promised to require supreme coordination. After dinner they repaired to the parlor, where Simanovitsch sat enchanted under the spell of Fox's conversation.

The tall, square-built American talked a mellifluous stream of American-accented French and German. He regaled Simanovitsch with stories from his native country with the fine expansiveness of the true raconteur. He had been born in Massachusetts but raised in France and Germany. He didn't relate just how he had come to be commissioned by George V, but Simanovitsch could easily imagine his worth to His Majesty's Secret Service. The man had command of six languages, a traveler's knowledge of India, Indochina, China, Japan, and Siberia, and was a fine hiker and well-versed in the military arts.

Simanovitsch met him the next morning for an early breakfast and the two embarked for Dresden to pick up the mannikins. Simanovitsch arranged to have the dummies shipped to Tiumen by a circuitous route. He and Fox left Germany that night, and in a week they had settled down at Tiumen.

Never in the history of the Russian monarchy had Siberia played host to a visit of the Imperial Family. The arrival of Nicholas and his family in Ekaterinburg caused a renewal of the conditions engendered by his previous stay at Tobolsk. Thousands upon thousands of churlish peasants, ambitious officers, and curious tradesmen milled around the village.

The crush and flux of this mass of humanity made the Bolsheviks' security job almost impossible. Not only were Fox and Simanovitsch able to slip in and out of the area undetected, but the arrival of the waxen cargo, in its seven separate pine boxes, went unnoticed.

Simanovitsch had no idea what the Bolsheviks were planning, so he assumed the worst. But even then, given the absolute confusion in the realm, he figured he had a month and a half to set up the rescue. He began at once.

When Simanovitsch summed up his impression of his partner, he didn't have to think too long to arrive at Fox's assignment. Fox had that peculiar American ambiguity to his countenance which comes of a multiple heritage and precludes any quick assignation of race. His lingual trademark, the Northern precision, could be turned on or off, depending upon whom he spoke to and his momentary whim. He spoke fluent French and had a working knowledge of Russian; these were the only two languages spoken in Siberia. If Fox played his cards right, he could easily infiltrate the regiment surrounding the Tsar. In fact, his superior cunning and great stature predisposed him to rise swiftly to the top of the tatterdemalion troops which the Bolsheviks had sent.

Fox, natively partial to the martial existence, jumped at the suggestion. Simanovitsch had clothes, papers, and other necessaries made up for his partner and gave him over to a friend, a junior officer, to give Fox the opportunity to accustom himself to the mores of the Bolshevik soldier.

Fox slipped into the regiment late that week. In two weeks he had the rank of captain nailed down and took charge of the immediate surveillance of the Imperial household.

Simanovitsch had planned to whisk out the Imperial Family from under the very noses of the soldiers by using the dummies as decoys. But when he saw how many soldiers manned the garrison, he deferred; subterfuge would not be enough. He would have to employ persuasion. He cabled to his bank in Novorossiisk for a million rubles. The job demanded no less.

Always preferring to begin at the top, Simanovitsch invited the commander of the garrison to dine with him at his lodgings. The fellow had been transferred from St. Petersburg, the social center of the nation, and had little to do after hours; he gladly accepted the invitation.

Simanovitsch brought up the best from his larder. The silver cutlery and crystal glassware reflected beams of lights from the candelabra. Creamy linen graced a table set with the choicest fruits, nuts, and vegetables of the province. The two dined on salmon and washed it down with pale yellow fruity wine. The commander didn't fail to notice the effort.

Simanovitsch didn't want to broach the subject of his concern unless he spoke to a thoroughly sober man, so he put his cards on the table early in the evening.

"This country seems so fresh," he said, "so wild and different from the plains of the West. I envy you your position, commander. What a pleasant way to spend one's time."

"Ah, yes, Simanovitsch," returned the commander, "the Siberian mountains and valleys and forests have a certain grandeur which those flat lands can never have. But I should be less ready to covet another man's situation until I discovered what his real chances were. My lot isn't so enviable as you would make it. Tonight I dine on linen; tomorrow morning I shall have my breakfast off a bare board."

"But surely," Simanovitsch rejoined, "such benefits as accrue to one from this dramatic and serene country make up for these minor inconveniences?"

"Yes, but one gets tired of hiking and hunting," said the commander with evident weariness in his voice. "One feels the necessity of some livelier pulse beating in one's blood than the beat of the wind on the pine, *n'est-ce pas?*"

"But are there not entertainments available in the towns?"

"If all one wishes is a giggling peasant girl, then, yes, you are right. But I miss the ladies of the winter circuit. Have you been in the capital for the winter season, Simanovitsch?" queried the commander. "Why, one's breath struggles with the dazzle of it all. That is what I miss, my friend, the chic."

"Yes," responded Simanovitsch. "I have been to the balls."

"And do you not feel the lack of them? Why, I don't know about all this revolution and fighting any more. One gets tired of it all after a time, Simanovitsch. But one must persist. There is no other way. Ah, but there were better times."

Simanovitsch found his mark. He took his glass, filled it with wine, and suspended it before his face just long enough to launch his opening volley.

"Commander, would you like three hundred thousand rubles in gold, and safe passage from Russia?"

"So that is your game, eh, Simanovitsch?" he smiled. "I knew there was something to all this. Go on. You interest me."

"Why, there isn't much further to go, Commander," Simanovitsch said, carefully measuring his words. "I'm sure you can divine the nature of my concern. It just needs to be said that you, too, can be transported—to Europe, like the Imperial Family."

"I see. And what do you wish me to do in your plan?"

"Why, we've no plan as yet," answered Simanovitsch. "But in any case, your part would not be very hard. Merely a looking away."

"And what about my men?" asked the commander. "There are two hundred men guarding that house. How shall you get around them?"

"There are never more than fifty or so on the immediate ground," returned Simanovitsch. "Of course, only the officers need be made sure of. That I was hoping to leave up to you."

"And how much are you willing to spend?"

"What I said before for you. Fifty thousand for the others."

"I see," said the commander. "You shall have to give me time."

Simanovitsch gave the commander a week to decide. He had great confidence that he had made the right move. On Friday he learned that he was right. The commander wished to dine with him again.

He opened their second meeting with a quick acceptance of Simanovitsch's offer, but he had long arguments against his scheme. Some of the officers were afraid. They wanted the money, but they feared what would happen to them if the Bolsheviks found them out. They would not have much use for rubles then.

Simanovitsch had thought about the same issue all week and had come up with a plan which he now described to the commander.

"My plan is simple," he began. "The family enters a convoy of trucks which pulls up to the house during the night. The trucks carry into the compound seven dummies which bear the likenesses of the family. These are brought inside and distributed to the various rooms. Human blood is also brought into the house. The trucks leave. An hour or so after they have left, a mock execution is carried out. Blood is splattered all over the wine cellar of the basement by your men. They spray the room with bullets. Meanwhile, I shall have my men obtain seven corpses, which can be burned as a subterfuge. You know the mine down the road a ways? That mineshaft seems the logical spot for a cremation.

"I have the brooches which Rasputin gave to the Tsar's daughters. These will go into the fire. When acid is poured over the embers, nothing will remain to identify them, except the brooches. Your men can claim an attempted escape had been perpetrated by agents of the White army. I happen to know that within two weeks, detachments will be within the region. Anyway, the dummies will be there as mute proof of some escape plan. They can claim that they had to execute them rather than let them fall into the enemy's hands—in essence, quite simple."

The commander took time to consider the proposal. There was one point which still irked him: "How do you propose to get these things into the house without the house guard discovering you and sounding the alarm prematurely?" he said.

"My dear commander," said the Jew, "the house guard is presently composed of eleven men. Their captain is a citizen of the United States and an agent of King George of England. Eight of the ten guards receive orders from me. The other two are dangerous, but they can be taken care of."

Shocked by this revelation, the commander coughed on his wine. When he had gained his breath he blurted out, "My God, Simanovitsch, but you do have your finger on things!"

Simanovitsch received this compliment with a graceful smile. "I have a great deal to work with," he stated.

By the middle of June all that remained was to set the date. Each man involved had received his detailed orders. The Imperial Family had been briefed. An itinerary had been selected. The trucks were gathered. The disguises for the family had been tailored. Papers were forged. Arrangements had been made at the local coroner's office to collect a pail of fresh human blood on the night of the escape. All was in readiness.

At ten-fifteen on the night of June 23, 1918, Charles James Fox was chatting with two of the men of his guard on the porch of the Ipatiev mansion. The night was hot and humid, and the men suffered from it in their heavy uniforms. Fox looked out into the gray twilight of the Siberian night.

"Damn hot," he muttered.

"Aye," returned one of the two soldiers. "You can feel the air at your throat."

Fox looked at his timepiece.

"Come on, then," he said, "we'll stop downstairs for a nip."

The three men entered the house and descended to the basement, where the wine cellar waited in cool darkness. Fox lighted a match and pretended to examine the labels for their vintage. He selected a bottle whose label had a small black dot in the upper left-hand corner. One of the soldiers lighted a candle; glasses and a corkscrew were found. Fox extracted the cork and poured a finger-full of the red liquid into each of the three glasses. The men all clicked them together in a toast and gulped them down—except for Fox, who carefully spit his to the floor. Seeing this, the other two opened their eyes in wide terror.

"Abominable year," Fox said.

Within a minute the two Bolsheviks were dead.

As Fox came up out of the basement, he could hear the low rumble of the truck convoy passing through the outer gate. He went upstairs to the bedroom where Nicholas and Alexandra had been waiting.

"They've come," he said. "Let's go—and be quiet about it."

The family gathered on the porch as three army trucks came around in a wide circle on the front lawn. The column halted before the house. Fox helped the seven members of the family, the doctor, and the single maid climb into the back of the middle truck.

The eight loyal members of the guard stowed their baggage in the truck. Then they unloaded the seven wrapped dummies from the second truck and distributed them in the various upper rooms. One man carried the pail of blood into the basement wineroom. Four of his buddies joined him. They carried the two Bolshevik's corpses out to the porch and put the bottle of wine and two glasses on the little table nearby.

As soon as the last box had been flung into the truck, Fox jumped into the cab and gave the leader the signal to proceed. At ten-forty the convoy passed through the gates on the first leg of a journey which would carry the Imperial Family through the Siberian wilderness south to Odessa and from there to their final destination, Poland.

About an hour after the trucks had left, the woods surrounding the Ipatiev house rang with the reports of rifle shots. A man splashed a pail of human blood on the floor of the wine room and hurried to the sink to wash out the bucket. The three men who had fired the shots then soaked their boots in the blood. The "execution" of the Imperial Family occurred at ten minutes to twelve.

Meanwhile, in a mineshaft a few miles away, Simanovitsch presided over an eerie bonfire. He threw certain effects of the Imperial Family into the pit: belt buckles, corset stays, earrings, necklaces, icons—and even the false teeth of the Tsar's physician, Dr. Eugene Botkin, and the corpse of "Jemmy," the pet Japanese spaniel of Anastasia. When the embers had ceased to glow, a couple of liters of sulfuric acid were poured over the ashes. Simanovitsch tossed a handful of jewels into the sizzling puddle of acid and mud.

"They were gifts from Rasputin," he said to no one in particular. "Even in death he serves his Tsar."

SIXTEEN

EPILOGUE

So ended the final chapter of Aaron Simanovitsch's life in Russia, but many of his subsequent exploits were to prove just as courageous and awesome.

Within a week after completing the final details of the escape, he left Ekaterinburg. He left the country only after smuggling out both his own and the Imperial Family's valuables, and after making sure that the family was cared for and their escape from Russia assured—an event which transpired successfully several months later. Simanovitsch then went to Germany where he established a new base of operations, more complex and expansive than the old one, with headquarters in Berlin and Paris. He commuted frequently between the two cities.

Nicholas and his family went to Poland. The Tsar felt that he wished to be close to his beloved Russia, especially since the White Russians seemed in a good position to defeat the Bolsheviks immediately after the 1917 Revolution. Because of the state secrets involved and the possibility of embarrassing repercussions from other governments involved, no government that participated in the escape volunteered or divulged information pertaining to the true nature of events.

But certainly, no one involved in the escape—and especially Simanovitsch—ever dreamed that the incident would remain unknown for more than half a century.

Early in 1919, Simanovitsch came to America for a twofold purpose. On the one hand, he wished to deposit vast sums of the

Tsar's money into several American banks and to negotiate for various diversified interests; on the other, he wished to leave some record of his accomplishments. As explained previously, he left behind him certain vital papers describing the nature and extent of his operations, with instructions to release this material if harm should befall him. He remained in America only six months, returning to Europe to continue his work as before.

Simanovitsch had gained such a favored position with the surviving Romanovs for having saved their lives and having assisted them so many times in the final days, that they enlisted his help in managing the entire Imperial fortune. It would not be stretching the imagination to suppose that Simanovitsch used a good portion of that money to his own advantage and to the advantage of the Jews. Innumerable Jewish businessmen and merchants had lost everything when the Bolsheviks gained power. We do know he was able to help many of his countrymen reestablish their businesses in their new homelands.

The next day after the "execution" at Ekaterinburg—and in all the years afterward—no bodies, bones, skulls, or dental work of members of the Imperial Family were ever found. In the months that followed, stories of their survival cropped up, in and out of Europe. In the midst of the developing mystery, two schools of thought were offered. First, that the Imperial Family had indeed been assassinated. This story was offered in a rather sketchy, melodramatic, and gory series of articles and subsequent book by Robert Wilton, a writer for the London Times. *The opposite view was given by Joseph Lasies, a French Army major and a correspondent in civilian life for the French newspaper* Le Matin. *He, too, wrote articles, and later a book, explaining his theory: the acid which supposedly dissolved the bones of the Imperial Family was, in fact, British diplomacy—which could, just as miraculously, make the Romanovs reappear whenever the British wanted them to.*

There were several official investigations, one by a White Russian judge, Nicholas A. Sokolov. The investigation concluded that the Romanovs had, indeed, been murdered. But his report, written in Russian, gained virtually no circulation in the West. Many of those who read it in French and German translations felt that there was no conclusive or substantiating evidence to support his findings. He had been assigned to close the imaginary coffin lid, and thus give Nicholas and his family better security in hiding.

As the 1940s passed with no Romanovs appearing on the scene, the assassination theory became the accepted one. Many people rightly asked: if the Romanovs had survived, then where were they now? And since there were no answers to be given, the establishment press concluded that they had, in fact, been killed.

Nicholas died in 1952 in the tiny village of Ciosaniec, Poland. A greater obscurity never enveloped the death of a figure so crucial to the course of Western civilization.

It wasn't until the middle 1960s that a large number of researchers, historians, scholars, and ex-diplomats banded together into a collective, fact-finding team to investigate the facts behind the Imperial Family's situation. Their findings revealed that five out of the seven Romanovs were still alive. The investigation and conclusions were published, with photos, in two books, Imperial Agent *(Devin-Adair Company) and* The Hunt for the Czar *(Doubleday), both by a foremost journalist, Guy Richards.*

But what of Aaron Simanovitsch? In 1941, a Gestapo agent came to Simanovitsch's door and seized him and his youngest son. Extensive investigation of concentration camp and Gestapo records have failed to uncover his name, and his death has never been established for certain. A life that raised many questions ends—in the public record—shrouded in similar mystery.

A SELECTED BIBLIOGRAPHY

Alexander, Grand Duke of Russia. *Once a Grand Duke.* New York: Cosmopolitan Book Corporation, Farrar and Rinehart, 1932.

Anastasia, Grand Duchess of Russia (Anna Anderson). *I Am Anastasia: The Autobiography of the Grand Duchess of Russia.* New York: Harcourt, Brace and Company, 1958.

Anastasia, Grand Duchess of Russia (Eugenia Smith). *Anastasia: The Autobiography of H. I. H. The Grand Duchess Anastasia Nicholaevna of Russia.* New York: Robert Speller and Sons, 1963.

Fülöp-Miller, René. *Rasputin, the Holy Devil.* New York: Garden City Publishing Company, 1928.

Gilliard, Pierre. *Thirteen Years at the Russian Court.* New York: Doran, 1921.

Maria, Grand Duchess of Russia. *Education of a Princess.* New York: The Viking Press, 1931.

Massie, Robert K. *Nicholas and Alexandra.* New York: Atheneum, 1967.

Obolensky, Prince Serge. *One Man in His Time.* New York: McDowell, Obolensky, 1958.

Purishkevich, Vladimir. *Comme J'ai Tué Raspoutine.* Paris: Povolozky, 1923.

Rasputina, Maria. *My Father.* London: Cassell, 1934.

Richards, Guy. *Imperial Agent: The Goleniewski-Romanov Case.* New York: Devin-Adair, 1966.

Richards, Guy. *The Hunt for the Czar.* Garden City, N.Y.: Double-day and Company, Inc., 1970.

Rodzianko, Michael. *The Reign of Rasputin.* London: Philpot, 1927.

Smythe, James P. *Rescuing the Czar,* Two Authentic Diaries Arranged and Translated by James P. Smythe, A.M., Ph.D. San Francisco: California Printing Company, 1920.

Sokolov, Nicholas. *Enquête Judiciaire sur l'Assassinat de la Famille Impériale Russe.* Paris: Payot, 1924.

Vorres, Ian. *The Last Grand Duchess: Her Imperial Highness Grand Duchess Olga Alexandrovna.* New York: Charles Scribner's Sons, 1965.

Vyrubova, Anna. *Memories of the Russian Court.* New York and London: Macmillan and Company, 1923.

Yusupov, Prince Felix. *Rasputin.* New York: Dial Press, 1927.

Yusupov, Prince Felix. *Lost Splendor.* Translated by Ann Green and Nicholas Katkov. New York: G. P. Putnam's Sons, 1954.

Index